Wok

WENDY SWEETSER

Wok

WENDY SWEETSER

NEW HOLLAND

First published in 2008 by
New Holland Publishers (UK) Ltd
London • Cape Town • Sydney • Auckland
Text and recipe copyright © 2008 Wendy Sweetser

Garfield House
86–88 Edgware Road
London W2 2EA
www.newhollandpublishers.com

Unit 1,
66 Gibbes Street
Chatswood, NSW 2067
Australia

80 McKenzie Street
Cape Town 8001
South Africa

218 Lake Road
Northcote, Auckland
New Zealand

Photographs copyright © 2008 New Holland Publishers (UK) Ltd
Copyright © 2008 New Holland Publishers (UK) Ltd

ISBN 978 1 84537 829 5

Commissioning editor: Clare Sayer
Copy-editor: Clare Hubbard
Design: Glyn Bridgewater
Photography: Ian Garlick
Food styling: Wendy Sweetser
Production: Marion Storz
Editorial Direction: Rosemary Wilkinson

Reproduction by Pica Digital PTE Ltd, Singapore
Printed and bound by Tien Wah Press, Malaysia

1 3 5 7 9 10 8 6 4 2

NOTE
The author and publishers have made every effort to ensure that all
instructions given in this book are safe and accurate, but they cannot accept
liability for any resulting injury or loss or damage to either property or
person, whether direct or consequential and howsoever arising.

Contents

Introduction

Cooks in the West have grown used to having different pans for different dishes, but in the East, particularly China, the wok has been a one-size-fits-all pan for over 2,000 years. This most versatile of cooking pots is commonly associated with stir-frying but, with a little experimentation, the home cook will soon discover it is equally useful for shallow-frying, deep-frying, making soups, braising, steaming and even smoking – in fact any dish cooked on a hob can be made in a wok. Invest in a good one and it could be the only pot you need.

Cooking in a wok is quick, healthy and fun and is especially suited to small households of one or two people. A wok might take up a lot of cupboard space in a tiny kitchen, but its versatility means you need fewer pans and, if you're on your own, you can put together a whole range of interesting meals from scratch quickly and with the minimum of hassle.

Tossing some fresh ingredients together in a wok will not only provide you with a tasty supper, it is also cheaper and more nutritious than relying on ready-meals and takeaways. Another bonus is that as most meals cooked in a wok are one-pot dishes, there is less washing-up too.

Wok cooking needs no special expertise, just a flexible wrist if you fancy emulating the chefs in your local Chinese restaurant with some serious stir-frying! It's also suitable for cooks of all ages including children who, as long as they're closely supervised, will not only enjoy using a wok but will also have a fun introduction to how to cook good food and eat proper meals.

WOK TRIVIA

If you thought a wok was just for cooking, then think again, as several years ago Stefan Raab, a German TV host and entertainer, dreamed up the idea of wok racing. His prototypes for both one- or four-person woksleds involved competitors strapping themselves into individually-crafted woks that were fitted to sleds so they could hurtle down special runs in the same way as the finest bob-sleigh teams. This new sport proved so popular that the first official Woksled World Championships were held in November 2003 and have been a regular feature of the annual alternative sporting calendar ever since.

Different types of wok

Originally there were just two types of wok – cast iron and carbon steel. Cast iron woks are heavy and hard-wearing and are used by Chinese cooks for stir-frying as they get very hot and stay hot for a long time. In fact in many Chinese restaurants it gets so hot when all the chefs are at work together that the fire pits or wok stoves must be surrounded by channels of cold water to cool things down.

In comparison carbon steel woks are lighter as the metal used to make them is beaten very thin. These woks are better suited to braising, steaming and deep-frying.

Today, the choice for the modern cook is much wider. Woks of all sizes and styles can be found in cookshops, ones made from stainless steel or anodized aluminium, others with a tough non-stick coating and even free-standing electric woks with their own stand designed to be used on a worktop without a hob in sight.

Choosing a wok

Woks come in many different sizes so pick one that suits your needs. A small, 30-cm (11½-in) diameter wok is fine if you're a household of one or two, but you'll need something bigger if you regularly cook for more people.

Two-handled woks are good for braising, deep-frying and steaming – those with a round-bottom are traditionally known as Cantonese woks. Two-handled woks with a flat bottom are an adaptation of the Cantonese wok, but redesigned to make them better suited to Western domestic cookers. Shanghai woks are similar to Cantonese woks, in that they also have two handles or 'ears', but they have a slightly deeper and rounder shape.

Woks with one long handle and a round base originate from northern China where they were used for stir-frying over fire pits. The long wooden or hollow metal handle is known as a pao: the word for the wrist-flicking action of tossing the stir-fried contents in a wok over the heat.

As with two-handled woks, single-handled ones have also been adapted to Western styles and are available

with either round or flat bottoms.

Traditional round-based woks are best suited to gas hobs as the flames can curl around the base and heat the wok evenly, whereas if they are used on an electric hob only a small part of the rounded base is in contact with the element.

Flat-based woks can be used on any kind of stove but they are particularly suited to electric, induction or ceramic hobs as their base covers the whole of the hot plate.

Cookshops, department stores and larger supermarkets all sell woks but they tend to be of the modern stainless steel or non-stick variety. These tend to be easier to look after, but if you're looking for something more traditional – and probably much cheaper – head to your nearest Chinese supermarket or food store.

Seasoning a wok

While stainless steel or non-stick woks only need to be washed before use, those made from carbon steel or cast iron must be 'seasoned' before they can be used for cooking. In ancient China the traditional way of seasoning a wok was to rub the inside of the wok with Chinese chives. Research by food historians has failed to uncover any scientific reason for why this worked, but maybe the coarse texture of the

chives was the closest thing to a modern scouring pad the local cooks were able to find.

To season a new carbon steel or cast iron wok today, wash it thoroughly to remove any residue of grease or dirt resulting from the manufacturing process and dry it thoroughly by wiping with absorbent kitchen paper. Place the wok over a medium heat and rub all over the inside with a pad of kitchen paper soaked in vegetable oil. Continue heating for about 5 minutes, greasing the wok once or twice more with the oil. (Take care when doing this.) Leave the wok to cool and it's now ready for use. Seasoning a wok helps it build up a natural non-stick surface, something that is lost if you scrub it clean with detergent.

If you don't use a carbon steel or cast iron wok regularly, smear the inside with a thin layer of oil before putting it away as this will prevent it from rusting. If your wok does develop rust, burn this off over a medium heat, reseason and it's ready to use again. With regular use the surface of the wok will blacken and develop a shiny patina – as the Chinese say 'the blacker the wok, the better the cook'.

Make sure you read and follow the instructions that come with your wok, as some manufacturers may give different instructions to those above.

Cleaning a wok

Stainless steel and non-stick woks can be washed after use like ordinary saucepans in hot water and detergent, but avoid using an abrasive scouring pad as this will scratch and damage the surface.

Carbon steel and cast iron woks should be washed in hot water without soap or detergent and wiped dry. If any food is badly burnt on to the surface of the wok, use a scouring pad or wire brush to remove the debris, then rinse with hot water and wipe clean.

Other useful equipment for wok cooking

Spatula

A wok spatula or chan is the traditional tool for tossing and lifting food while stir-frying. Its slightly curved edge follows the rounded shape of the wok so you can pull up and toss the ingredients on the bottom of the pan – something that would be much more difficult with a large spoon or fish-slice. The traditional chan is made of metal but if your wok has a non-stick coating use a wooden one instead, as the shovelling action used when stir-frying will damage the surface.

Lid

For braising, stewing, steaming or smoking foods it is essential to have a domed lid that will fit snugly over your wok and prevent liquid evaporating or steam escaping during cooking. If your wok doesn't come with its own lid it's worth buying one as it is much easier and safer to pop a lid on than try and cover the wok with foil.

Tempura rack

Another useful accessory is a tempura rack, which is a semi-circular rack that fits over one side of the wok and is used to drain and keep foods warm that are being deep-fried in the wok in batches. The rack can also be used for steaming small quantities of food, such as vegetables that are to be added to a soup, or to braise ingredients being cooked in the wok that need only brief cooking.

Bamboo baskets

Lidded Chinese bamboo baskets (available in various sizes) or a round rack that fits into the top of the wok are useful for steaming larger quantities of food. The baskets can be stacked on top of each other on a trivet, and the strips of bamboo that form the base of each basket are spaced sufficiently apart to allow steam to pass from one basket to the next without creating condensation that would make items such as wontons soggy.

Wok burner

A wok burner is a metal ring perforated with large holes that can be used on a conventional hob or a barbecue to hold the wok firmly in place. The ring keeps the wok stable when dishes such as braises or soups are being left to cook and is essential when cooking any dish that involves shallow-frying, deep-frying or the pre-cooking of vegetables or noodles in boiling water.

Tongs and mesh strainer

A pair of long-handled barbecue-style tongs or a Chinese mesh strainer is useful for draining food from hot oil or liquid where some of the ingredients in a dish require less cooking time than others and need to be removed from the wok before the dish is ready.

Ladle

A ladle is a convenient way to add ingredients to the wok or transfer a cooked dish from the wok to a serving plate. If you calculate the capacity of your ladle you can also use it as a quick way to measure stock and other liquids.

Chopsticks

Chinese cooks rarely use forks or spoons when they cook as they prefer to mix, stir or add ingredients to a wok using a pair of long chopsticks. The chopsticks are also handy when you want to taste food to check for seasoning. They also make excellent tongs for removing food from the wok – once you've mastered the art of getting a grip on slippery ingredients!

Cooking in a wok

Stir-frying

When most of us think of a wok we think of stir-fried food; certainly the rounded base of a wok makes it the perfect shape for stir-frying, as ingredients can be tossed and turned over easily so that they cook evenly.

The secret of a successful stir-fry is to do all of the chopping, mixing, crushing and measuring before you start cooking. Cut vegetables into even, one-bite-sized pieces and add them gradually to the wok according to the cooking time they need. Denser vegetables – such as carrots, onions and broccoli – should be added to the wok first, followed by ones that need only medium cooking – such as peppers, celery and baby corn. Finally those that simply need a 'flash in the pan' – such as bean sprouts, fine asparagus spears and shredded spring onions – can be dropped in and tossed over the heat for a few minutes at the end.

Stir-frying over a high heat will ensure vegetables stay crisp while they brown, but if your recipe requires the vegetables to soften without browning, lower the heat to medium.

Meat should be sliced across the grain and stir-fried quickly over a high heat to ensure it seals quickly and stays tender.

Shallow-frying

A wok can be used in the same way as a frying pan to shallow-fry ingredients. Heat just enough oil to cover the base of the wok before adding the ingredients to be fried and flip over halfway through cooking so that both sides are sealed and browned.

Deep-frying

A wok makes an excellent deep-fryer as long as certain safety precautions are followed. When deep-frying, don't fill more than one-third of the wok with oil and once all the food has been cooked, leave the hot oil – either in the wok or in another suitable container – in a safe place to cool down.

Any food for deep-frying needs a protective coating of batter or breadcrumbs to protect it from the hot oil and it's important to heat the

17

oil to the correct temperature so the food begins cooking immediately. If the oil is too cool, too much will be absorbed by the food and instead of crisp, light morsels the food will be soggy, greasy and heavy. If you don't have a cooking thermometer, a cube of bread dropped into the oil will sizzle and start to brown after 40 seconds when the oil is at a temperature of 180°C (350°F), or after 30 seconds at 190°C (375°F).

Steaming

A wire rack, Chinese bamboo basket or heatproof plate placed on a trivet in the wok can all be used to steam food. Once the food is ready to be steamed, cover the wok tightly with a lid and use stock flavoured with herbs, spices or Oriental sauces to add flavour.

Braising

A wok can also be used for braising food in a sauce. First seal the meat or poultry in a little oil over a high heat before adding the other ingredients and then cover the wok with a lid for the remainder of the cooking time.

Smoking

Smoking food is another thing you can do in a wok. Start by lining the wok with a large sheet of foil, leaving extra to hang over the side, then put in the smoking mixture and set a metal rack in the wok about 5 cm (2 in) above the mixture. Place the food to be smoked on the rack, spacing it out evenly, and cover the wok with a lid. Fold the extra foil over the lid to make a tight seal and place the wok over a high heat until you can smell (but not necessarily see) smoke. Reduce the heat and leave the food to smoke for the time specified in the recipe until it is cooked through.

SAFETY FIRST
Because of their unique shape both round-bottomed and flat-bottomed woks can be dangerously unstable if left unattended on a conventional hob. When stir-frying, hold the handle of the wok to keep it steady and use a wok burner when shallow frying, deep-frying or if leaving a dish to simmer, braise, smoke or steam.

Marinating foods

Leaving meat, poultry or fish to steep in a mix of herbs, spices and bottled sauces helps them absorb the diverse flavours of the marinade. To cook, lift the food from the marinade and add it to the wok but don't throw the marinade away. Any marinade left can be added to the wok as a sauce, but it's important to boil it so that any potentially harmful bacteria is killed off before the sauce is spooned over the finished dish.

When marinating, cover and refrigerate the ingredients for the time specified in the recipe. Meat and poultry will benefit from long marinating of several hours or overnight; fish and seafood should only be marinated for an hour or so otherwise their delicate flesh will start to lose flavour.

Ingredients for wok cooking

Storecupboard ingredients

Lots of recipes that are cooked in a wok call for Oriental or Mediterranean ingredients, so it's worth stocking up on some or all of the following:

- Soy sauce (light and dark)
- Teriyaki sauce
- Thai fish sauce. Used in marinades, dipping sauces and dressings, it has a pungent, salty flavour. Fish sauce is regularly used in Thailand, Vietnam and the Philippines in the same way that soy sauce is used in China.
- Chilli sauce (sweet and hot)
- Vinegar (rice, cider, wine, balsamic)
- Oil (mild flavoured oil such as groundnut, sunflower or vegetable; extra-virgin olive oil, ordinary olive oil, sesame oil)

- Oyster sauce. A thick stir-fry sauce made from ground oysters, water, cornflour, caramel and salt. Once the bottle has been opened, it must be kept in the fridge or the sauce will turn mouldy.
- Stir-fry sauces (black bean, plum, sweet and sour)
- Chinese/Japanese cooking wine (mirin, Shao Xing or use dry sherry)
- Spices (coriander, saffron, cumin, chilli powder, Chinese five spice, ginger)
- Tinned coconut milk
- Hoisin sauce. A dark, thick, sweet sauce made from soya beans, spices and garlic, also know as Chinese Barbecue Sauce.
- Dried Chinese mushrooms. These need to be soaked in warm water for about 30 minutes before cooking. The soaking water makes a good stock for adding to a dish but strain it first to get rid of any grit that might have been trapped in the mushrooms.
- Jars of fresh purées (lemon grass, ginger, garlic)

- Rice (basmati, long-grain, Thai sticky)
- Noodles (dried egg noodles, dried rice noodles, mung bean, soba, udon or buy fresh as needed from Asian food stores). Sold both dried and fresh and can be made from wheat, buckwheat, mung bean or rice flours. Shown in the picture above are fresh udon noodles (top) and bottom (left to right) dried medium flat rice (pad Thai) noodles, dried soba noodles and dried rice stick noodles.
- Tinned bamboo shoots
- Tinned water chestnuts

21

Fresh ingredients

- Root ginger. Fresh root ginger is fibrous to eat so needs to be peeled and grated or very finely chopped before being added to a dish (see opposite, bottom left).
- Lemon grass stalks
- Garlic
- Red and green chillies. Red chillies are ripened green chillies but both can be equally fiery. As a general rule, the smaller the chilli the hotter it will be. When preparing chillies, take care to protect your hands either by wearing thin rubber gloves or by washing them thoroughly immediately afterwards and never touch your face or eyes as they can give nasty, stinging burns.
- Mushrooms. Hundreds of different types of mushrooms grow in South East Asia such as the tiny pinhead enoki mushrooms from Japan (see opposite, bottom right), shiitake, straw mushrooms and shimeji (see opposite, top left).
- Herbs and greens: coriander, chives, parsley, thyme, basil, pak choi (see opposite, top right)
- Bean sprouts
- Limes
- Spring roll wrappers

A note on seasoning

Where salt is important to the taste of a finished dish it is included in the ingredients list but, with so many of us watching our salt intake these days, in the majority of recipes it is left to individual cooks to season dishes according to personal taste. Also, many ready-made stocks and Oriental sauces contain quite high levels of sodium so adding extra salt is unnecessary. If you are trying to cut back on salt, it's worth buying low salt soy sauce as it contains around 40 per cent less salt than standard soy sauce.

Which oil to use?

In most recipes in the book particular oils are specified, but unless the flavour of an oil really is crucial to the finished dish – for example extra-virgin olive oil or toasted sesame oil – these can be varied according to what you have available. Sunflower, grapeseed, vegetable, corn and groundnut oils all have a mild, non-invasive flavour and are interchangeable in most dishes.

FISH
AND
SHELLFISH

Cod Provençal

The warm flavours and colours of Mediterranean vegetables and herbs transform plainly-cooked cod fillets into something special. Aïoli, the garlicky Provençal mayonnaise, could be served as an accompaniment.

Serves 4

- 4 × 150-g (5-oz) cod fillets, skinned
- 1 tsp paprika
- 1 tsp herbes de Provence
- 4 tbsp extra-virgin olive oil
- 1 red pepper, deseeded and cut into wedges
- 1 yellow pepper, deseeded and cut into wedges
- 1 courgette, sliced
- 2 garlic cloves, peeled and thinly sliced
- 4 small tomatoes or 8 cherry tomatoes, halved
- 4 anchovy fillets, snipped into small pieces
- 75 g (3 oz) black olives
- Juice of 1 lemon
- Few fresh basil leaves, shredded
- Freshly ground black pepper

1 Dust the cod fillets with the paprika and dried herbs and set aside.

2 Heat half the oil in a wok and fry the red and yellow pepper wedges, the courgette slices and garlic over a medium-high heat for 6–8 minutes or until lightly browned.

3 Add the tomatoes and stir-fry for a further 2 minutes. Remove from the wok and keep warm in a low oven.

4 Heat the rest of the oil in the wok, add the cod and scatter over the chopped anchovies and black olives. Fry over a medium heat for 5 minutes, then carefully turn the fish over and fry for a further 3–4 minutes or until cooked.

5 Divide the vegetables between serving plates and top with the cod, anchovies and olives. Stir the lemon juice into the wok and as soon as it bubbles, spoon the cooking juices over the fish.

6 Garnish with the shredded basil, season with black pepper; serve with new or sauté potatoes.

> You can use other fish fillets instead of cod, but adjust the cooking time according to the thickness of the fillets.

Fragrant Steamed Seafood

This mouthwatering selection of seafood needs little accompaniment beyond a salad of shredded vegetables – cucumber, carrots and white radish would all work well. Cut the vegetables into strips and toss with a light dressing.

Serves 4

- 8 raw king prawns, peeled and deveined, tails left on
- 8 scallops, roes removed
- 225 g (8 oz) squid, cleaned
- 4 spring onions, trimmed
- 300 ml (½ pt) fish stock
- 1 small knob fresh root ginger, peeled and sliced
- 1 red chilli, deseeded and halved
- 250 g (9 oz) mussels in their shells (see page 46 for preparation)
- 2 tbsp chopped fresh coriander

Sauce

- 2 tbsp light soy sauce
- 1 tsp caster sugar
- 150 ml (¼ pt) coconut milk

> **Discard any mussels that remain closed after cooking**

1 Arrange the prawns, scallops and squid on a steaming rack and tuck the spring onions between them. Pour the fish stock into a wok and add the ginger and chilli. Add the mussels to the wok, position the rack on top and scatter over the chopped coriander.

2 Bring the stock to a simmer, put the lid on and steam the seafood for about 5 minutes or until the prawns have turned pink, the scallops and squid are tender and the mussel shells have opened.

3 Remove the seafood from the rack, cutting the squid into bite-sized pieces. Drain the mussels from the cooking liquor and keep everything warm in a low oven.

4 Strain the liquid from the wok, reserving 150 ml (¼ pt). Pour this back into the wok, add the soy sauce and sugar, stir in the coconut milk and heat through. Divide the seafood between serving dishes and serve with the sauce spooned over.

Seared Mullet with Herby Vegetables

Colourful and aromatic with flavours of citrus and fresh herbs, this Mediterranean-style dish makes a satisfying lunch or supper for two.

Serves 2

- 4 tbsp extra-virgin olive oil
- 2 carrots, peeled and cut into julienne or thinly sliced
- 150 g (5 oz) tenderstem broccoli
- 1 courgette, cut into julienne or thinly sliced
- 1 tsp fresh thyme leaves
- 4 red mullet fillets (see box below)
- Juice of 1 lime
- 2 tbsp chopped fresh parsley

> **If red mullet is not available, trout, sea bass or cod fillets could be used instead. Adjust the cooking time for the fish according to the thickness of the fillets.**

1 Heat half the oil in a wok and stir-fry the carrots and broccoli over a high heat for 3 minutes. Add the courgette and thyme and stir-fry for 2 minutes. Drain the vegetables from the wok, pile on to two serving plates and keep warm in a low oven.

2 Add the remaining oil to the wok and when it is really hot, put in the mullet fillets skin-side down. Seal them over a high heat for 2 minutes, then flip the fillets over and cook for a further 1 minute. Sprinkle with the lime juice and scatter over the parsley.

3 Lift the fish from the wok and arrange two fillets on top of each pile of vegetables. Spoon over any juices left in the pan and serve immediately.

Creole prawns with feta

This winning combination of succulent prawns, sharp feta cheese and tomato and herb sauce is a version of the popular Greek taverna dish – oven-baked prawns with feta. Serve it with crusty bread to mop up the rich tomatoey juices.

Serves 2

- 2 tbsp olive oil
- 2 shallots, peeled and chopped
- ½ green pepper, deseeded and chopped
- 1 tsp paprika
- 350 ml (12 fl oz) tomato pasta sauce
- 2 tsp chopped fresh oregano
- 2 tbsp ouzo (see box below)
- 8 large, raw prawns
- 100 g (4 oz) feta cheese, crumbled
- Freshly ground black pepper
- 2 tbsp chopped fresh parsley

1 Heat the oil in a wok and fry the shallots and green pepper over a medium heat for 5 minutes. Sprinkle over the paprika, cook for 1 minute, then stir in the tomato sauce, oregano and ouzo. Simmer for 5 minutes.

2 Peel and devein the prawns, leaving the tails on or removing them as preferred. Add the prawns to the wok and scatter over the feta cheese.

3 Cover with a lid and simmer gently for about 8–10 minutes or until the prawns turn pink and the cheese starts to melt. Grind over plenty of black pepper, scatter over the parsley and serve.

> **Ouzo will give the sauce a mild aniseed flavour, so if that's not to your liking, you can easily substitute brandy or orange juice, or just leave it out altogether.**

Scallop and Vegetable Stir-fry

This mouthwatering combination of baby scallops and fresh vegetables makes the ideal supper dish when you're short of time. Serve on its own or with Thai steamed rice.

Serves 2

- 2 tbsp vegetable oil
- 2 celery sticks, sliced
- 4 spring onions, trimmed and sliced
- 100 g (4 oz) button mushrooms, halved
- 75 g (3 oz) sugar snap peas, sliced
- 1 tsp grated root ginger or 1 tsp ginger purée
- 1 garlic clove, peeled and finely chopped
- 350 g (12 oz) queen scallops
- 150 ml (¼ pt) fish or vegetable stock
- 1 tsp cornflour
- 2 tbsp light soy sauce

1 Heat the oil in a wok, add the celery, spring onions, mushrooms, sugar snap peas, ginger and garlic and stir-fry over a medium-high heat for 4–5 minutes until the vegetables are almost tender. Remove and set aside.

2 Add the scallops and stir-fry for 2 minutes. Remove and set aside.

3 Mix the stock with the cornflour until smooth and add to the wok with the soy sauce. Stir over the heat until the sauce thickens, return the vegetables and scallops to the wok and heat through for 1 minute. Serve immediately.

Small queen scallops are quick to cook and have a delicate, sweet flavour making them ideal for stir-fries. If they're unavailable, larger scallops can be used: slice them in half through the middle before cooking.

Clams with Lemon Grass, Garlic and Coriander

Sweet, juicy clams cooked with fragrant Asian herbs and spices makes a delicious meal – perfect for eating outdoors on a summer's day. Serve with French bread.

Serves 4

- 1.1 kg (2½ lb) clams in their shells
- 1 tbsp vegetable oil
- 1 red onion, peeled and finely chopped
- 1 stick of lemon grass, finely sliced
- 2 fat garlic cloves, peeled and finely chopped
- 100 ml (4 fl oz) dry white wine
- 175 ml (6 fl oz) fish stock
- 3 tbsp chopped fresh coriander
- Freshly ground black pepper

1 Wash the clams thoroughly in plenty of cold water.

2 Heat the oil in a wok and fry the onion over a low heat for 5 minutes, stirring frequently. Add the lemon grass and garlic and fry for a further 3 minutes.

3 Add the clams, pour over the wine and stock and cover the wok with a lid. Cook for 5 minutes or until all the clam shells have opened. Discard any that remain closed.

4 Pile the clams into serving bowls, draining them from the wok with a large slotted spoon. Pour the cooking juices over the clams, sprinkle with the coriander and season with freshly ground black pepper.

Any clams that stay closed after cooking must be discarded as they won't be safe to eat.

Potato Rösti with Gravlax and Soured Cream

Crisp potato nests topped with strips of gravlax and a spoonful of sharp soured cream make an unusual starter or hot two-bite nibble to serve with drinks.

Makes 12

- 250 g (9 oz) potatoes, peeled
- 2 spring onions, trimmed and finely chopped
- 1 large egg, beaten
- Freshly ground black pepper
- Vegetable oil for frying
- 175 g (6 oz) gravlax, thinly sliced and cut into strips
- 4 tbsp soured cream
- Dill sprigs to garnish

1 Grate the potatoes into a bowl. Cover with cold water and leave to stand for 1 hour.

2 Drain the grated potato and dry thoroughly on absorbent kitchen paper. Rinse and dry the bowl and return the potato to it. Mix in the spring onions, beaten egg and season with freshly ground black pepper.

3 Heat 2.5 cm (1 in) of oil in a wok and carefully add 4 tablespoons of the potato mixture, spacing each tablespoon well apart. Fry for 2–3 minutes over a medium-high heat or until crisp and golden brown, turning the potatoes over halfway through cooking if necessary. Drain on kitchen paper and cook eight more rösti in the same way.

4 Allow the rösti to cool slightly, then top each one with gravlax and a teaspoonful of soured cream. Garnish with small sprigs of dill, season again with pepper and serve immediately.

> **Instead of gravlax, the rösti could be topped with strips of smoked salmon if you prefer**

Prawns with Minted Chilli and Orange Sauce

Large, raw prawns are perfect for stir-frying, as keeping them moving over a high heat means they're much less likely to overcook and toughen as on a barbecue or under a grill. They are cooked once they have turned evenly pink all over.

Serves 2

- 1 bunch of fresh coriander
- 2 garlic cloves, peeled and roughly chopped
- 1 tsp grated root ginger or ginger purée
- 3 tbsp vegetable oil
- 350 g (12 oz) large, raw prawns, peeled, with tails left on
- 150 ml (¼ pt) fresh orange juice
- 2 tbsp light soy sauce
- 1 tsp cornflour
- 1 red chilli, deseeded and finely sliced
- 1 tbsp chopped fresh mint
- 75 g (3 oz) green beans, halved lengthways
- 100 g (4 oz) small Asian mushrooms (e.g. shimeji or enoki) or baby button mushrooms
- 3 cherry tomatoes, halved

1 Remove any tough stalks from the coriander and put the rest of the bunch in a food processor with the garlic, ginger and 1 tablespoon of the oil and blend to a smooth purée. Spread the coriander mixture over the prawns and leave to marinate in the fridge for 1 hour.

2 In a small bowl, mix together the orange juice, soy sauce and cornflour until smooth. Stir in the chilli and chopped mint. Set aside.

3 Heat the remaining oil in a wok, add the green beans and mushrooms stir-fry over a high heat for 3 minutes. Add the prawns and any marinade left in the dish and stir-fry for 2 minutes. Add the cherry tomatoes and stir-fry for a further 1 minute or until the prawns turn pink.

4 Pour in the orange sauce mixture and stir until thickened. Simmer for 30 seconds and serve immediately with rice.

Look out for boxes of Asian mushrooms in your local supermarket. Most are sold still joined at the roots in clumps, so the caps and stems need cutting off with scissors or a sharp knife before cooking.

Mediterranean Fish Stew

This quick-to-cook dish is full of wonderful colours and flavours. Use a mixture of different white fish, such as cod, snapper and monkfish, or just one variety as you prefer.

Serves 4

- 2 tbsp olive oil
- 1 red onion, peeled and chopped
- 2 garlic cloves, peeled and chopped
- ½ green pepper, deseeded and chopped
- 1 courgette, chopped
- 350 g (12 oz) potatoes, peeled and cut into chunks
- Few strands of saffron
- 1 tsp smoked paprika
- 150 ml (¼ pt) dry white wine
- 400-g (14-oz) tin chopped tomatoes
- 1 tbsp shredded fresh basil
- 500 g (1 lb 2 oz) white fish fillets, skinned and cut into 2.5-cm (1-in) pieces
- 225 g (8 oz) raw prawns, peeled
- Salt and freshly ground black pepper

1 Heat the oil in a wok, add the onion and fry gently for 5 minutes. Add the garlic, green pepper, courgette and potatoes and fry for a further 5 minutes, stirring occasionally.

2 Crumble the saffron over the vegetables and add the smoked paprika. Fry for 2 minutes, then add the wine, tomatoes and basil. Simmer for 15 minutes or until the potatoes are almost tender, the tomatoes have reduced and the sauce thickened.

3 Add the fish and prawns and season to taste. Simmer for a further 5 minutes until all the fish is cooked. Serve immediately.

> **Smoked paprika is made from the sweet red peppers grown in Spain's Estremadura region, which are smoked and then ground to a fine powder. Known locally as 'red gold', this aromatic spice adds a warm, smoky flavour to dishes.**

Garlic and Chilli Seafood with Vegetable Ribbons

A variation on the popular Spanish tapas dish, where prawns are seared quickly in hot olive oil and garlic and carried, still sizzling, to the table in an earthenware dish. Add extra garlic and dried chillies for more spice if you wish.

Serves 4

- 2 courgettes
- 2 large carrots
- 6 tbsp olive oil
- 350 g (12 oz) raw prawns, peeled, but tails left on
- 8 scallops
- 3 garlic cloves, peeled and chopped
- ½ tsp crushed, dried chillies

It's important not to overcook the seafood as it will quickly become tough and tasteless. Once the prawns turn pink they're ready and whilst scallops need to be cooked through, they should still be moist and juicy in the centre.

1 Trim the courgettes, peel the carrots and shave both vegetables into long, wafer-thin slices by drawing the peeler down their length.

2 Heat 2 tablespoons of the oil in a wok, add the courgette and carrot ribbons and toss over a brisk heat for 1–2 minutes until starting to soften. Drain from the wok and keep warm.

3 Add the rest of the oil to the wok and add the prawns, scallops, garlic and dried chillies. Stir-fry for a couple of minutes over a fairly high heat until the prawns turn pink and opaque.

4 Divide the vegetable ribbons between serving plates and pile the prawns and scallops on top, spooning over any juices left in the wok. Serve immediately.

Jumbo Prawn Toasts with Sesame, Ginger and Chilli

Serve these as an appetizer with pre-dinner drinks accompanied by a small bowl of soy sauce or plum sauce for dipping, or as a starter, garnishing each serving with a small salad.

Makes 16

- 16 raw jumbo prawns, peeled, with heads removed but tails left on
- 2 eggs
- 4 tbsp cornflour
- 2 tbsp sesame seeds
- 1 tsp ginger purée
- 2 tbsp sweet chilli sauce
- 4 large slices of white bread, crusts removed
- Vegetable oil for frying
- 2 tbsp chopped fresh Chinese chives or ordinary chives

1 Cut down the back of each prawn, about three-quarters of the way through the flesh, and devein by pulling out the dark thread running down the prawn's length. Place the prawns on a board, open each one out like a butterfly and flatten gently.

2 Beat the eggs with 2 tablespoons of the cornflour in a shallow dish until evenly mixed. Beat in the sesame seeds and ginger.

3 Cut each slice of bread into four triangles. Dip the triangles into the egg mixture so they are well coated on one side, letting the excess drip off back into the bowl, and place them, dipped side up, on a board. Dust the prawns with the rest of the cornflour and gently press a prawn, cut side down, on each triangle of bread.

4 Heat 2.5 cm (1 in) of oil in a wok until hot and fry the triangles, three or four at a time, for about 1 minute or until the bread is golden brown and the prawns pink. Drain on absorbent kitchen paper and serve hot, sprinkled with the chives.

The prawns need to be pressed gently so the egg sticks them on to the bread triangles and they don't fall off into the oil during frying.

Prawn and White Fish Masala

Cod, tilapia, monkfish or any other thick-fleshed white fish would be suitable for this mild curry, which needs no accompaniments beyond a crusty baguette or a flatbread, like naan, to mop up any juices.

Serves 4

- 2 tbsp sunflower oil
- 1 red onion, peeled and thinly sliced
- 250 g (9 oz) potatoes, cut into even-sized pieces and boiled until just tender
- 1 courgette, sliced
- 100 g (4 oz) mushrooms, sliced or quartered
- 2 tbsp tikka masala curry paste
- 200 ml (7 fl oz) fish stock
- 2 tbsp tomato purée
- 4 tbsp thick, natural yogurt
- 1 tsp cornflour
- 225 g (8 oz) raw tiger prawns, peeled
- 350 g (12 oz) white fish fillet, skinned and cubed

1 Heat the oil in a wok and gently fry the onion for 5 minutes until softened. Add the potatoes, courgette and mushrooms and fry for a further 5 minutes.

2 Stir in the curry paste, add the stock and tomato purée and bring to a simmer. Cover the wok and cook gently for 10 minutes.

3 Mix the yogurt and cornflour together, take the wok off the heat and stir the yogurt mixture into the sauce. Return the wok to the heat and bring the sauce back to a simmer, stirring constantly. Add the prawns and fish and simmer uncovered for 5 minutes until the prawns turn pink and the fish is cooked. Serve immediately.

> **If using fish with delicate flesh, such as cod or haddock, avoid stirring the sauce too much as the cubes will break up. Monkfish, with its firm flesh, is ideal as the pieces tend to stay whole.**

Mussels with White Wine, Shallots and Cream

Rinse the mussels in cold water to remove any sand or bits of shell. Discard any with open shells that don't close when tapped, as the mussels inside won't be safe to eat, and pull out any tough fibrous 'beards' trapped between the shells.

Serves 4

- 4 shallots, peeled and chopped
- 2 fat garlic cloves, peeled and thinly sliced
- 6 tbsp chopped fresh parsley
- 200 ml (7 fl oz) dry white wine
- 150 ml (¼ pt) cold water
- 2 kg (4½ lb) mussels in their shells (see above for preparation)
- 2 tbsp double cream or crème fraîche
- Salt and freshly ground black pepper
- Warm crusty bread to serve

Mussels need a large wok with a wide base. If too tightly packed, the ones at the bottom will overcook before those on top are ready.

1 Put the shallots, garlic, 2 tablespoons of the parsley, wine and the cold water in a wok and bring to the boil. Lower the heat and leave to bubble gently for 5 minutes.

2 Increase the heat under the wok so the liquid boils, add the mussels and cover with a lid. Cook for about 5 minutes, shaking the wok regularly until all the mussel shells have opened. Discard any that remain closed.

3 Lift out the mussels with a slotted spoon and pile into four warm serving bowls. Boil the liquid in the wok for 2–3 minutes, then remove from the heat and whisk in the cream and seasoning to taste.

4 Spoon the sauce over the mussels, sprinkle with the rest of the parsley and serve straight away with plenty of warm crusty bread to soak up the delicious juices.

Salt and Pepper Squid with Chilli Mayonnaise

Squid is sweet and tender when lightly cooked, but soon goes tough if you leave it in the pan for too long. Here the crunchy-coated squid is served with a spicy mayonnaise, but sweet chilli sauce or soy sauce could be used instead.

Serves 2 (or 4 as an appetizer)

Chilli mayonnaise
• 4 tbsp lemon mayonnaise
• 1 tsp chilli sauce

Squid
• 350 g (12 oz) squid, cleaned
• 4 tbsp plain flour
• ½ tsp salt
• ½ tsp freshly ground black pepper
• Vegetable or sunflower oil for frying

Garnish
• 2 spring onions, shredded
• 1 red chilli, deseeded and very finely chopped

1 Stir the mayonnaise and chilli sauce together in a small bowl, cover with cling film and chill in the fridge for several hours to allow the flavours to develop.

2 Slice half the squid bodies into rings. Cut the rest into small pieces and, using a sharp knife, score the inner side in a criss-cross pattern, taking care not to cut all the way through the flesh. Cut any tentacles into short lengths. Mix the flour, salt and pepper together on a plate and dust the squid until well coated. Leave on the plate for 10 minutes then dust again, adding more flour if necessary.

3 Heat about 4 cm (1½ in) of oil in a wok to 180°C (350°F) (or until a small cube of bread browns in 40 seconds) and fry the squid, in batches if necessary, for about 2 minutes or until lightly golden. Drain on kitchen paper and serve hot with the spring onions and red chilli sprinkled over. Serve with the mayonnaise.

Heat the oil to the correct temperature so the squid cooks quickly and doesn't become chewy.

Red-braised Fillets of Sea Bass

Frying or grilling whole freshwater carp and then 'red-braising' it in a sweet-sour sauce is a popular fish dish in China. Fillets of other fish can be cooked in the same way, such as a red snapper, sea bream, sea bass or trout.

Serves 4

- 1 tsp ginger purée
- 1 garlic clove, peeled and crushed
- 1 tbsp light soy sauce
- 1 tbsp rice wine or dry sherry
- 1 tsp sweet chilli sauce
- 3 tbsp yellow bean sauce
- 100 ml (3½ fl oz) fish stock
- 1 tsp brown sugar
- 4 x 175-g (6-oz) sea bass fillets
- 2 tbsp groundnut or sunflower oil
- 2 tsp sesame oil

To garnish
- 1 large carrot, peeled and cut into julienne
- 2 spring onions, shredded
- 1 tbsp tinned bamboo shoots, shredded
- 2 tbsp snipped fresh chives

1 In a small bowl, mix together the ginger, garlic, soy sauce, rice wine or sherry, chilli sauce, yellow bean sauce, fish stock and sugar, stirring until the sugar dissolves and the ingredients are evenly mixed.

2 Rinse the fish fillets and pat dry with absorbent kitchen paper. With a knife, cut several slashes through the skin of each fillet.

3 Heat the oil in a wok, add two fillets skin-side down and cook over a medium heat for 3 minutes. Turn them over and cook for a further 1 minute, then drain and set aside. Cook the other two fillets in the same way and set aside.

4 Sprinkle the fish with the sesame oil. Pour the sauce mix into the wok and bring to a simmer. Return the fish to the wok, basting the fillets with the sauce. Cook gently for 5 minutes, turning the fish over halfway or spooning the sauce over the fillets regularly.

5 Serve garnished with the shredded vegetables and chives and accompany with egg noodles or rice.

Slashing the skin of the fish helps the fillets absorb flavour from the braising sauce.

51

Seared Scallops with Warm Papaya and Mango Salad

This makes a great quick lunch or supper dish – or a starter for a more formal dinner, in which case leave the scallops to marinate for an hour in the lime and honey mixture before cooking. Prawn crackers make an easy accompaniment.

Serves 4

- 8 large or 12 small scallops
- Juice of 1 large lime
- 3 tbsp light soy sauce
- 1 tsp clear honey
- ½ tsp ginger purée
- 2 tbsp sunflower oil
- ½ red pepper, deseeded and sliced
- 4 spring onions, sliced
- 75 g (3 oz) bean sprouts
- ½ papaya, peeled, deseeded and chopped
- 1 small mango, peeled and flesh chopped
- 50 g (2 oz) wild rocket

1 Place the scallops in a bowl. Mix together the lime juice, soy sauce, honey and ginger and pour over the scallops, turning them over so they are well coated.

2 Heat 1 tablespoon of oil in a wok and stir-fry the red pepper for 2 minutes over a brisk heat. Add the spring onions and bean sprouts and stir-fry for 2 minutes. Add the papaya and mango and stir until the fruit is evenly mixed with the vegetables. Heat through for 1 minute, then tip everything out of the wok on to a plate and keep warm in a low oven.

3 Add the remaining oil to the wok, drain the scallops from the lime and soy marinade, reserving the marinade, and add them to the wok. Fry for 1–2 minutes on each side until the scallops are golden, then drain.

4 Place the rocket on four serving plates and top with the vegetables, fruit and scallops. Pour the reserved marinade into the wok, bring to the boil and then spoon over the salads. Serve immediately.

To prepare a mango, use a small, sharp knife to cut the flesh away from either side of the fibrous stone in two thick slices. Peel off the skin and chop the mango flesh, cutting off any extra left clinging to the stone.

Salmon Steamed with Lemon Grass, Lime and Basil

The aromatic seasonings add an Oriental twist to the salmon, complementing its rich flesh perfectly. Serve with steamed Thai rice or a dish of vermicelli rice noodles tossed with shredded spring onions and a finely chopped red chilli.

Serves 4

- 4 x 150-g (5-oz) salmon fillets
- 1 small knob of root ginger, peeled and cut into fine shreds
- 1 stalk of lemon grass, quartered lengthways
- 2 tbsp chopped fresh basil
- Finely grated zest of 1 lime
- About 450 ml (¾ pt) fish stock or water
- 4 spring onions, trimmed
- 200 g (7 oz) tenderstem broccoli
- 1 carrot, peeled and cut into julienne

Sauce
- 2 tbsp Thai fish sauce
- 1 tsp light brown sugar
- 2 tbsp light soy sauce
- Juice of 1 lime
- ½ stalk of lemon grass, finely sliced

1 Place the salmon fillets on to a steaming rack and sprinkle over the ginger, lemon grass, half the basil and lime zest.

2 Pour the stock into the wok so it is one-third full. Tuck the spring onions, broccoli and carrot around the salmon on the rack. Bring the stock to a simmer, cover the wok with a lid and steam for 10 minutes or until the salmon flesh flakes easily and the vegetables are cooked.

3 For the sauce, mix all the ingredients together, stirring until the sugar dissolves. Place the salmon and vegetables on serving plates and drizzle over the sauce. Garnish with the rest of the chopped basil.

Thai basil, also known as 'holy basil', is an Asian variety of the more familiar sweet basil that is widely used in Mediterranean dishes. Thai basil has a distinctive flavour of mild basil and aniseed and small, deep green oval leaves with purple flowers and stems. More difficult to track down than sweet basil, it can be found in Oriental stores, but use either basil for this recipe.

Lemon, Parsley and Chive Sardines

Any small fish could be cooked in this way – anchovies would work well – but ask the fishmonger to scale, clean and remove the heads for you. Serve the sardines plain with lemon wedges, or with mayonnaise or tartare sauce.

Serves 4

- 2 eggs
- 175 g (6 oz) fresh breadcrumbs
- 2 tbsp finely chopped fresh parsley
- 1 tbsp finely chopped fresh chives
- Finely grated rind 1 lemon
- Freshly ground black pepper
- 12 sardines, split open and filleted (see box below)
- 4 tbsp plain flour
- Vegetable oil for frying
- Lemon wedges to serve

1 Beat the eggs together in a shallow dish. Mix the breadcrumbs with the parsley, chives and lemon rind, season with plenty of freshly ground black pepper and spread out on a large plate.

2 Dust the sardines with the flour, dip in the beaten egg and then cover the sardines with the crumb mixture until both sides of the fish are well coated.

3 Heat about 1 cm (½ in) of oil in a wok and, when hot, shallow-fry the sardines in batches for 1–2 minutes on each side until golden and crisp. Drain from the wok on to a plate lined with absorbent kitchen paper and serve hot with lemon wedges.

> To fillet sardines, cut them along the underside and lay them skin-side up, opening them out. With your thumbs, press down the backbone of each fish to loosen it, then turn the fish over and snip the backbone just above the tail with kitchen scissors. Work one end of the backbone loose and gently pull it away from the flesh – it will come out in one piece with the ribs attached.

Prawn, Spinach and Carrot Stir-fry

Quick to prepare and so good to eat! Succulent prawns and crisp vegetables make this tasty stir-fry an extremely satisfying meal for two.

Serves 2

- 350g (12oz) raw prawns, peeled
- 2 tbsp rice vinegar
- 1 tbsp Thai fish sauce
- 2 tbsp light soy sauce
- 1 garlic clove, peeled and chopped
- 1 tsp grated root ginger or ginger purée
- 1 tbsp groundnut oil
- 2 carrots, peeled and cut into julienne
- 100g (4oz) mushrooms, sliced
- 1 courgette, cut into julienne
- 150g (5oz) baby spinach leaves

If baby spinach leaves are not available, mature leaf spinach can be used – but make sure any tough stalks are cut away before shredding the leaves

1 Place the prawns in a bowl. Mix together the rice vinegar, fish sauce, light soy sauce, garlic and ginger with 1 tablespoon of water and pour over the prawns, stirring until they are coated. Cover and leave to marinate in a cool place for 1 hour.

2 Drain the prawns, reserving the marinade. Heat the oil in a wok. When it is hot, add the carrots and stir-fry over a high heat for 2 minutes. Add the mushrooms and courgette and stir-fry for a further 2 minutes. Remove all the vegetables from the pan and set aside.

3 Add the prawns and stir-fry for 3 minutes. Return the carrots, mushrooms and courgette to the wok, add the spinach and pour in the reserved marinade.

4 Toss everything together over the heat for 2-3 minutes until piping hot and the spinach has wilted.

POULTRY

Stir-fried Chicken with Almonds

Whole almonds give a pleasing crunch to this easy stir-fry and they provide a good contrast to the tender chicken and crisp vegetables. Serve with boiled rice.

Serves 4

- 3 tbsp groundnut oil
- 75 g (3 oz) whole almonds
- 4 boneless, skinless chicken breasts, diced
- 1 red onion, peeled and finely sliced
- 1 carrot, peeled and thinly sliced
- 1 celery stick, sliced
- 1 green pepper, deseeded and chopped
- 75 g (3 oz) tinned bamboo shoots, sliced if large
- 2 tsp sweet chilli sauce
- 2 tbsp light soy sauce
- 1 tsp cornflour
- 175 ml (6 fl oz) chicken stock

> **For vegetarians – cut firm tofu into 2-cm (¾-in) cubes and lightly fry until golden just like the chicken.**

1 Heat 1 tablespoon of the oil in a wok and stir-fry the almonds for about 30 seconds until lightly browned. Remove and set aside.

2 Add another tablespoon of the oil to the wok and stir-fry the chicken over a fairly high heat for 5 minutes or until golden. Remove and set aside.

3 Add the remaining tablespoon of oil and stir-fry the onion and carrot for 3 minutes. Add the celery, green pepper and bamboo shoots and stir-fry for a further 3 minutes.

4 Return the almonds and chicken to the wok with the chilli sauce. In a small bowl, whisk the soy sauce together with the cornflour and add the stock. Pour into the wok and toss the ingredients over the heat for 2–3 minutes until the sauce is bubbling.

Steamed Chicken with a Warm Balsamic Dressing

A light but tasty way to cook chicken that's ideal for a summer lunch, especially if you're watching the calories. The longer you can leave the chicken to marinate, the more flavours it will absorb.

Serves 4

- 4 boneless, skinless chicken breasts
- 1 tsp clear honey
- 2 tbsp balsamic vinegar
- 2 garlic cloves, peeled and crushed
- 1 tsp finely chopped root ginger or ginger purée
- 1 tbsp fresh thyme leaves
- 4 medium tomatoes, halved
- 100 g (4 oz) green beans, trimmed
- 1 courgette, cut into long slices on the diagonal
- 300 ml (½ pt) chicken stock
- 2 tbsp snipped fresh chives

> **Making cuts in the chicken breasts helps the flavours of the marinade permeate right through the flesh.**

1 Make several cuts across each chicken breast with a sharp knife and lay side by side in a shallow dish. Mix together the honey, balsamic vinegar, garlic, ginger and thyme and pour over the chicken, turning the breasts so they are coated in the marinade. Cover and leave in the fridge for 2 hours or longer.

2 Lift the chicken from the marinade (reserving the marinade) and place on the steaming rack of a wok. Arrange the tomato halves, green beans and courgette slices around the breasts. Pour the stock and marinade into the wok, position the rack on top and cover with a lid. Steam for 15 minutes or until the chicken is cooked through.

3 Transfer the chicken and vegetables to serving plates, spoon over the cooking juices and scatter over the chives. Slice the chicken through the cuts you made previously and serve with new potatoes.

Mini Barbecued Duck Rolls

Crisp, two-bite rolls that make a great party nibble. Hoisin – also know as Chinese barbecue – sauce, gives the duck and vegetable filling a sweet, spicy flavour.

Makes 16 rolls

- 2 duck breasts, with skin
- 600 ml (1 pt) chicken stock
- Vegetable oil for frying
- ½ red pepper, deseeded and finely chopped
- 1 celery stick, finely chopped
- 75 g (3 oz) shiitake mushrooms, finely chopped
- 75 g (3 oz) bean sprouts
- 1 tbsp finely chopped celery leaves
- 3 tbsp hoisin sauce
- 1 tbsp rice vinegar
- 16 x 12.5-cm (5-in) square Chinese spring roll wrappers
- 1 egg white, lightly beaten

1 Place the duck in a wok, pour over the stock to cover. Put the lid on and cook gently for 45 minutes. Leave the duck to cool in the stock, then lift it out, skin, and shred the meat. Pour off the stock.

2 Dry the wok. Add 2 tablespoons of oil and stir-fry the pepper and celery over a medium heat for 3 minutes. Add the mushrooms, bean sprouts and leaves and stir-fry for 3 minutes. Add the duck, hoisin and vinegar and cook for 1 minute. Leave to cool. Wash and dry the wok.

3 Place a spring roll wrapper on a board and top with a spoonful of the duck mixture. Brush the edges with egg white and roll up around the filling, pressing the edges together to seal completely. Repeat with the remaining wrappers and filling.

4 Heat 2.5 cm (1 in) of oil in a wok and fry the rolls in two batches until golden brown (about 5 minutes). Drain and serve hot with extra hoisin sauce for dipping.

Plum Duck with Stir-fried Vegetables

The wonderful combination of sweet-sour Asian flavours provides a mouthwatering sauce for duck and stir-fried vegetables. Serve spooned over egg noodles, plain boiled rice or fried rice.

Serves 2

- 2 duck breasts, skinned if preferred (see box below)
- Freshly ground black pepper
- 2 tbsp groundnut oil
- 1 carrot, peeled and sliced
- 4 spring onions, trimmed and sliced
- 100 g (4 oz) baby corn, chopped
- 100 g (4 oz) mushrooms, sliced
- 4 cherry tomatoes, halved
- 1 tbsp light soy sauce
- 3 tbsp stir-fry plum sauce
- 1 tbsp rice vinegar
- 1 tsp sesame seeds

> **If you prefer to skin the duck breasts before cooking, you'll need to brush them with a little oil before adding them to the wok.**

1 Season the duck with freshly ground black pepper. Heat a wok over a medium heat, add the duck and cook for 7–8 minutes or until the breasts are done to your liking, turning them over once or twice.

2 Drain the duck from the wok and set aside for 5 minutes before slicing as thinly as possible. Pour off the fat and carefully wipe out the wok with absorbent kitchen paper.

3 Heat the oil in the wok, add the carrot and stir-fry over a medium-high heat for 3 minutes. Add the spring onions, corn and mushrooms and stir-fry for 3 minutes. Add the cherry tomato halves and stir-fry for a further 2 minutes.

4 Combine the soy sauce, plum sauce and rice vinegar and pour over the vegetables. Add the duck and toss everything over the heat for 1–2 minutes until coated in the sauce. Serve at once with the sesame seeds scattered over.

Spiced Chicken with Cider and Mustard Sauce

Creamy mustard sauce spiked with cider, apple and fresh sage then tossed with spicy chicken makes a deliciously different main course. Serve with sauté potatoes and a green vegetable such as broccoli or sugar snap peas.

Serves 4

- 50 g (2 oz) butter
- 2 tbsp caster sugar
- 2 dessert apples, cored and cut into wedges
- 4 boneless, skinless chicken breasts or 8 chicken thighs
- 2 tsp ground coriander
- 2 tbsp sunflower oil
- 1 courgette, chopped
- 300 ml (½ pt) dry cider
- 1 tbsp wholegrain mustard
- 2 tbsp apple sauce
- 300 ml (½ pt) chicken stock
- 1 tbsp cornflour
- 150 ml (¼ pt) double cream
- 2 tsp chopped fresh sage

1 Heat the butter in a wok and when it has melted, stir in the sugar. Fry the apples wedges until golden on each side. Remove and set aside.

2 Carefully wipe out the wok with kitchen paper. Dust the chicken with the coriander. Heat the oil in the wok and fry the chicken over a fairly high heat for 3 minutes until lightly browned.

3 Lower the heat, add the courgette and fry for 2 minutes. Add the cider, mustard, apple sauce and stock and bring to a simmer. Cover with a lid and cook gently for 15 minutes.

4 Mix the cornflour with the cream and stir into the sauce with the sage. Bring back to a simmer, stirring constantly, and then cook uncovered for a further 5 minutes. Add the caramelized apple slices and heat through for 1–2 minutes.

Apples with firm, fairly tart flesh, such as Cox or Granny Smith, don't need to be peeled before caramelizing them in butter and sugar.

Chicken, Bacon and Fennel Pan-fry

A great brunch dish for when you fancy a lazy weekend with family or friends. Par-boiling the potatoes in their skins speeds up the cooking time without sacrificing any of their flavour.

Serves 4

- 500 g (1 lb 2 oz) small new potatoes
- 4 tbsp sunflower oil
- 3 boneless, skinless chicken breasts, cut into chunks
- 4 rashers of back bacon, chopped
- 1 tsp paprika
- 1 head of fennel, thinly sliced
- ½ red pepper, deseeded and chopped
- Freshly ground black pepper
- 2 tbsp snipped fresh chives

Fennel adds a light aniseed flavour to the pan-fry but if you prefer, add 100 g (4 oz) baby button mushrooms to the wok with the red pepper instead.

1 Boil the potatoes in a covered pan of water for 5 minutes (you can use a wok for this as long as it is flat-bottomed or you have a wok burner for it). Drain and when cool enough to handle, cut each potato in half, or bite-sized pieces as necessary. Carefully dry the wok.

2 Heat 2 tablespoons of the oil in the wok, add the chicken breasts and bacon and stir-fry over a fairly high heat for 4–5 minutes until browned. Remove and set aside.

3 Add the rest of the oil to the wok, put in the potatoes and sprinkle over the paprika. Fry over a medium heat until the potatoes are just starting to brown, stirring occasionally. Add the fennel and red pepper and fry for 5 minutes.

4 Return the chicken and bacon to the wok and fry, stirring frequently, for 2 minutes. Serve seasoned with freshly ground black pepper and the chives scattered over.

Kung Po Chicken

Cooking from Sichuan in western China is hotter and spicier than the sweet-sour stir-fries of Cantonese cuisine, and this combination of stir-fried chicken, chillies and peanuts is one of the region's most popular dishes.

Serves 2

- 2 boneless, skinless chicken breasts, cut into small chunks
- 2 tsp grated root ginger or ginger purée
- 1 tbsp light soy sauce
- 1 tsp cornflour
- 4 spring onions
- 2 tbsp groundnut oil
- 100 g (4 oz) unsalted, unroasted peanuts
- 3 dried red chillies, deseeded and chopped
- ½ tsp caster sugar
- 2 tsp rice vinegar

1 Put the chicken in a bowl. Whisk together the ginger, soy sauce and cornflour until smooth, pour over the chicken and stir until evenly coated. Set aside in fridge to marinate for at least 1 hour.

2 Trim the spring onions. Remove the green tops from two of them and chop finely. Slice the rest of these two onions, and the other two whole ones, into 2.5-cm (1-in) lengths.

3 Heat the oil in a wok and stir-fry the peanuts over a high heat for 1 minute or until golden. Drain the nuts from the wok with a slotted spoon and set aside.

4 Lower the heat to medium-high, add the chicken with its marinade and sliced spring onions and stir-fry for 3 minutes. Add the nuts and chillies, sprinkle over the sugar and rice vinegar and toss together over the heat for 2 minutes.

5 Sprinkle over the chopped spring onion tops and serve at once with rice or egg noodles.

The dried chillies make this a pretty hot dish so reduce the quantity if you prefer or add 1 medium red chilli, deseeded and very finely chopped.

Braised Turkey with Mushrooms

**A light main meal that could be made with
boneless chicken breasts instead of turkey if you prefer.
A selection of baby vegetables such as carrots and corn
makes the perfect accompaniment.**

Serves 2

- 2 tbsp sunflower oil
- 350 g (12 oz) turkey breast slices
- 1 red onion, peeled and chopped
- 100 g (4 oz) mushrooms, sliced
- 150 ml (¼ pt) chicken stock
- 1 tsp tomato purée
- 150 ml (¼ pt) dry white wine
- 50 g (2 oz) frozen peas
- 1 tsp cornflour
- 4 tbsp soured cream
- 1 tbsp chopped fresh parsley

> The cornflour thickens the sauce a little and it also stabilizes the soured cream, preventing the sauce from separating once the cream has been added.

1 Heat the oil in a wok and fry the turkey slices over a high heat until browned on both sides. Remove from the wok and set aside.

2 Lower the heat, add the onion and mushrooms and fry for 5 minutes. Add the stock, tomato purée, wine and frozen peas and bring to a simmer.

3 Return the turkey to the wok, cover and cook over a low heat for 10 minutes. In a small bowl, stir the cornflour into the soured cream and add to the wok. Stir until evenly blended in, bring back to a simmer and cook for a further 2 minutes.

4 Sprinkle over the parsley, and serve with new potatoes and vegetables of your choice.

Jamaican Chicken with Gungo Peas and Yam

A spicy dish from the Caribbean that's hot, hot, hot! If you think your taste buds won't be able to stand the heat, use a mild curry paste and go easy on the pepper sauce. Serve with rice sprinkled with chopped, fresh coriander.

Serves 4

- 2 tbsp vegetable oil
- 1 onion, peeled and chopped
- 1 green pepper, deseeded and chopped
- 250 g (9 oz) yam, peeled and cut into small pieces
- 2 garlic cloves, peeled and finely chopped
- 4 boneless, skinless chicken breasts, cut into small chunks
- 3 tbsp hot curry paste
- Few drops of hot pepper sauce (or to taste)
- 230-g (8-oz) tin chopped tomatoes
- 150 ml (¼ pt) chicken stock
- 400-g (14-oz) tin gungo peas, drained and rinsed

1 Heat the oil in a wok, add the onion and fry over a low heat until softened. Add the pepper, yam and garlic and fry for 5 minutes, stirring occasionally.

2 Stir in the chicken, curry paste and pepper sauce until the chicken and vegetables are coated in the paste, then pour in the tomatoes and stock. Cover with a lid and simmer for 15 minutes.

3 Stir in the gungo peas, re-cover the wok and simmer for a further 15–20 minutes or until the yam is tender.

If you can't find yam, orange-fleshed sweet potato could be used instead. Black-eyed beans could also be added instead of gungo peas.

Duck with Maple and Chilli Glaze

A deliciously different way to serve duck that combines East-West flavours to perfection. Serve the duck sliced as thinly as possible, accompanied by Egg Fried Rice with Bacon, Peppers and Peas (see page 144) or plain boiled rice.

Serves 4

- 4 duck breasts, with skin
- 4 tbsp maple syrup
- 2 tsp chilli sauce
- 4 tbsp dark soy sauce
- 1 tsp grated root ginger or ginger purée
- Juice of 2 oranges
- Shredded spring onions, celery, red chilli and radish to serve

Leaving the duck breasts to stand will make them easier to carve. After standing, transfer the breasts to a board and slice thinly across the meat using a sharp, thin-bladed knife.

1 Place the duck skin-side up in a shallow dish. Mix together the maple syrup, chilli sauce, soy sauce and ginger and spoon over the duck. Cover and place in the fridge to marinate for 2 hours or longer.

2 Heat a wok until hot. Lift the duck breasts out of the dish, reserving the marinade. Add the duck to the wok, skin-side down and cook over a fairly high heat until brown. Turn the breasts over, lower the heat and cook for a further 5–10 minutes or until done to your liking.

3 Remove the duck breasts from the pan to a plate and leave in a warm place to rest for 5 minutes. Tip off excess fat from the wok, add the orange juice and marinade and boil, stirring, for 1 minute.

4 Carve the duck as thinly as possible and serve with the pan juices spooned over. Garnish with the shredded vegetables and chilli.

Coconut and Coriander Chicken

The province of Goa on India's west coast is famous for the sweet, juicy coconuts that grow there in profusion. Coconut milk is added to many local dishes and this recipe is a treat for lovers of spicy dishes who don't like them too hot.

Serves 4

- 2 tbsp vegetable oil
- 1 red onion, peeled and finely chopped
- ½ aubergine, chopped into small pieces (see box below)
- 1 red pepper, deseeded and chopped
- 4 boneless, skinless chicken breasts, cut into bite-sized pieces
- 2 tbsp mild curry paste (e.g. korma)
- 1 tbsp tomato purée
- 300 ml (½ pt) coconut milk
- 4 tbsp chopped fresh coriander

1 Heat the oil in a wok, add the red onion and fry over a low heat for 5 minutes until softened.

2 Add the aubergine and red pepper and fry for 5 minutes, stirring frequently. Add the chicken and fry for a further 5 minutes until the vegetables are tender and the chicken lightly browned.

3 Stir in the curry paste and tomato purée until the vegetables and chicken are coated, then pour in the coconut milk. Simmer gently for 5 minutes.

4 Sprinkle over the coriander and serve immediately with boiled rice.

If you have time, you can sprinkle the aubergine pieces with salt and leave them to stand for 30 minutes, before rinsing and cooking. The salting process draws out excess water and reduces the amount of oil the aubergine flesh absorbs as it cooks.

Hot and Sour Soup with Chicken and Dumplings

Clear broths form an important part of a meal in Asian countries like China, Japan and Thailand, where they are served as a palate cleanser between courses that have stronger flavours.

Serves 4

- 40 g (1½ oz) dried Chinese mushrooms
- 900 ml (1½ pt) chicken stock
- 1 stalk of lemon grass, finely chopped
- 1 tsp ginger purée or grated root ginger
- 3 tbsp Thai fish sauce
- Juice of 2 limes
- 2 red chillies, deseeded and finely sliced
- 1 boneless, skinless chicken breast, cut into bite-sized pieces
- 1 head of pak choi, shredded
- 12 Chinese dumplings
- 2 spring onions, shredded

1 Put the dried mushrooms in a bowl, pour boiling water over to cover and leave them to soak for 30 minutes until tender.

2 Bring the stock to the boil in a wok. Add the lemon grass and ginger and simmer gently for 5 minutes. Add the fish sauce, lime juice and half the sliced chillies and simmer for 3 minutes.

3 Drain the dried mushrooms and strain the soaking liquid into the broth. Add the chicken, mushrooms and pak choi and carefully drop in the dumplings one at a time. Simmer gently for 10 minutes until the dumplings are cooked.

4 Serve the soup sprinkled with the spring onions and the rest of the sliced chillies.

> **If you don't have an Oriental food store nearby, add 12 peeled, raw tiger prawns to the soup instead of dumplings and replace the dried mushrooms with 75 g (3 oz) fresh shiitake or whatever mushrooms are available.**

Turkey Meatballs in a Rich Tomato Sauce

The meatballs can be served with pasta, rice or mashed potatoes and will be a popular dish with all the family. To save time, make up double quantities of the meatballs and sauce and freeze half for another meal.

Serves 4

- 450 g (1 lb) turkey mince
- 1 tbsp fresh thyme leaves
- 2 garlic cloves, peeled and crushed
- 2 tsp Dijon mustard
- 50 g (2 oz) fresh breadcrumbs
- 1 egg, beaten
- 2 tbsp sunflower oil
- 2 rashers of back bacon, chopped
- ½ red pepper, deseeded and chopped
- 2 x 400-g (14-oz) tins chopped tomatoes
- 2 tbsp tomato purée
- 150 ml (¼ pt) red wine or chicken stock
- Salt and freshly ground black pepper

1 In a large bowl, mix together the turkey mince, half the thyme, garlic, mustard and breadcrumbs. Stir in the beaten egg and, with damp hands, roll the mixture into about 24 walnut-sized balls.

2 Place the meatballs on a plate in a single layer, cover with cling film and chill in the fridge for 1 hour or longer.

3 Heat the oil in a wok, add half the meatballs and fry over a medium heat until evenly browned all over. Lift out of the wok with a draining spoon and fry the rest of the meatballs in the same way.

4 Add the bacon to the wok and fry until lightly browned. Add the red pepper, tomatoes, tomato purée and wine or stock and season to taste. Return the meatballs to the wok, lower the heat, cover and simmer for 20 minutes. Serve with the rest of the thyme sprinkled over.

Cantonese Chicken with Pineapple and Lychees

A favourite sweet and sour dish given a new look with the addition of lychees and pineapple. If you like things hot, add a finely chopped red chilli to the pan with the ginger. Serve with boiled rice or vermicelli rice noodles.

Serves 4

Batter

- 100 g (4 oz) self-raising flour
- ½ tsp salt
- ½ tsp baking powder
- 250 ml (8 fl oz) light lager

Sauce

- 150 ml (¼ pt) chicken stock
- 2 tbsp rice vinegar or white wine vinegar
- 1 tbsp light brown sugar
- 3 tbsp light soy sauce
- 2 tbsp tomato ketchup
- 2 tsp cornflour

Chicken

- Vegetable oil for frying
- 450 g (1 lb) skinless, boneless chicken breasts, cut into small chunks
- 4 tbsp plain flour
- 1 green pepper, deseeded and cut into small chunks
- 1 tsp ginger purée
- 8 spring onions, cut into 2.5-cm (1-in) lengths
- 8 lychees, peeled and stones removed if fresh
- 1 pineapple ring, cut into chunks

Leaving the batter to stand for an hour before using allows the gluten in the flour to swell, giving a lighter, crisper result. If, after standing, you find the batter has become too thick, stir in a little water or extra beer.

1 To make the batter, sift the flour, salt and baking powder into a large bowl. Make a well in the centre and pour in half the lager. Whisk until smooth and then gradually whisk in the rest of the lager to make a batter. Leave to stand, covered, for 1 hour before using.

2 To make the sauce, put all but a couple of tablespoons of the stock, the vinegar, brown sugar, soy sauce and ketchup into a wok and heat gently until the sugar dissolves. Stir the cornflour into the remaining stock, add to the wok and stir continuously over a low heat until the sauce has thickened. Simmer for 1 minute, then pour into a bowl and set aside. Wash the wok and dry with absorbent kitchen paper.

3 To cook the chicken, heat about 4 cm (1½ in) oil in the wok to 180°C (350°F) (or until a small cube of bread browns in 40 seconds). Dust the chicken pieces with the flour, dip them in the batter and deep-fry in batches in the hot oil until golden brown and crisp. Drain them on to a plate lined with absorbent kitchen paper and keep warm in a low oven.

4 Carefully pour most of the oil out of the wok into a heatproof bowl and leave in a safe place to cool, leaving about 2 tablespoons of oil in the wok.

5 Reheat the oil, add the pepper and ginger and stir-fry for 3 minutes. Add the spring onions, lychees and pineapple and stir-fry for 1 minute. Return the chicken to the wok, pour in the sauce and stir everything together until the chicken and vegetables are coated.

6 Simmer for 1 minute and serve immediately.

Lemon, Honey and Ginger Chicken

This aromatic stir-fry can be served with plain rice or egg noodles, but if you're cooking to impress, Egg Fried Rice with Bacon, Peppers and Peas (see page 144) makes a colourful accompaniment.

Serves 4

- 2 tbsp vegetable oil
- 50 g (2 oz) unsalted cashews
- 2 tsp cornflour
- 2 tbsp light soy sauce
- Juice of 1 lemon
- 1 tsp ginger purée
- 1 tbsp clear honey
- 150 ml (¼ pt) chicken stock
- 4 skinless, boneless chicken breasts, cut into strips
- 1 large carrot, cut into julienne
- 100 g (4 oz) mangetout, sliced lengthways
- 4 spring onions, trimmed and sliced
- 50 g (2 oz) bean sprouts

Remove the cashews from the wok just before they look sufficiently golden as they'll darken on standing.

1 Heat half the oil in a wok and stir-fry the cashews until golden. Drain them from the pan with a slotted spoon and set aside.

2 In a small bowl, whisk together the cornflour, soy sauce, lemon juice, ginger, honey and stock until smooth.

3 Add the rest of the oil to the wok and, when hot, add the chicken and stir-fry for 5–6 minutes over a brisk heat until golden brown. Remove and set aside.

4 Lower the heat under the wok to medium, add the carrot, mangetout, spring onions and bean sprouts and stir-fry for 3 minutes. Stir in the soy sauce mix and bring to a simmer, stirring constantly until the liquid is thickened and smooth.

5 Return the chicken to the wok and simmer for 2 minutes. Add the cashews, simmer for 1 minute and then serve immediately.

Chicken with Orange and Tarragon Sauce

The chicken breasts are simmered in a crème fraîche sauce, flavoured with orange, wholegrain mustard and the mild aniseed of tarragon. A perfect special-occasion dish that is ready in minutes.

Serves 4

- 2 tbsp sunflower oil
- 4 skinless boneless chicken breasts
- 2 carrots, peeled and cut into julienne
- 1 small leek, trimmed and thinly sliced
- 175 ml (6 fl oz) fresh orange juice
- 4 tbsp crème fraîche
- 2 tsp wholegrain mustard
- 1 tbsp chopped fresh tarragon
- Orange wedges and tarragon sprigs to garnish

1 Heat the oil in a wok, add the chicken breasts and fry for about 10 minutes over a fairly high heat until they are browned on both sides and cooked through (see box below). Remove and set aside.

2 Add the carrots and leek to the wok and fry gently for 2 minutes. Stir in the orange juice, crème fraîche, mustard and tarragon and bring to the boil. Simmer for 2 minutes, then return the chicken to the wok and heat through for 1 minute.

3 Serve the chicken with the sauce spooned over, piling the carrots and leek on top. Garnish with orange wedges and tarragon sprigs.

> **Start the chicken breasts off over a higher heat so they seal quickly, then turn the heat down a little to finish cooking them – the time they take will vary according to the thickness of the meat.**

Red Pesto Chicken with Olives

Pesto – made from pounded garlic, pinenuts, Parmesan and basil – gives dishes a wonderfully aromatic flavour. Red pesto has tomato and chilli mixed in, adding colour and a touch of spice to this creamy chicken dish.

Serves 4

- 2 tbsp olive oil
- 4 boneless, skinless chicken breasts
- ½ red pepper, deseeded and chopped
- ½ yellow or orange pepper, deseeded and chopped
- 1 courgette, sliced or cut into julienne
- 2 garlic cloves, peeled and crushed
- 100 ml (3½ fl oz) dry white wine
- 150 ml (¼ pt) chicken stock
- 3 tbsp sun-dried tomato purée
- 2 tbsp red pesto
- 4 tbsp crème fraîche or double cream
- Salt and freshly ground black pepper
- 12 black olives
- Handful of fresh basil leaves

1 Heat the olive oil in a wok and brown the chicken breasts, two at a time, on both sides over a fairly high heat. Remove them from the wok and set aside.

2 Add the peppers, courgette and garlic to the wok and stir-fry for 5 minutes until starting to soften. Pour in the wine and let it bubble for 1 minute, then stir in the stock, tomato purée and red pesto.

3 Return the chicken to the wok, lower the heat, cover and simmer for 15 minutes or until the breasts are cooked through.

4 Stir in the crème fraîche or double cream and season to taste. Serve with the olives and basil leaves scattered over.

If you buy olives preserved in oil they can be added straight to the chicken. If they are preserved in brine, rinse and pat them dry with absorbent kitchen paper first.

MEAT

Five Spice Steak with Peppers

Five spice mix – a blend of star anise, cinnamon, Sichuan pepper, cloves and fennel – is an important ingredient in Chinese cooking as the spices are believed to provide the perfect ying-yang balance of sweet, sour, bitter, salty and hot.

Serves 4

- 2 tbsp vegetable oil
- 500 g (1 lb 2 oz) rump steak, cut into thin strips
- 1 red onion, peeled and thinly sliced
- 1 onion, peeled and thinly sliced
- 1 red pepper, deseeded and thinly sliced
- 1 green pepper, deseeded and thinly sliced
- 1 yellow pepper, deseeded and thinly sliced
- 2 garlic cloves, peeled and finely chopped
- 1 tsp Chinese five spice powder
- 150 ml (¼ pt) beef stock
- 1 tsp cornflour
- 2 tbsp dark soy sauce

1 Heat half the oil in a wok and stir-fry the steak in two batches over a high heat for 3–4 minutes or until browned. Remove from the wok and set aside.

2 Lower the heat to medium-high, add the rest of the oil and stir-fry the onions for 3 minutes. Add the peppers and the garlic and stir-fry for 3 minutes.

3 Return the steak to the wok, sprinkle in the five spice powder and stir-fry for 1 minute. Mix the stock and cornflour together until smooth, pour into the wok and add the soy sauce. Stir-fry for 1 minute until the sauce bubbles and coats the meat and vegetables. Serve immediately.

> **Instead of using the three peppers, you could substitute 1 large carrot cut into julienne, 1 chopped courgette and 100 g (4 oz) baby corn.**

Chilli Bean Beef with Nachos and Cheese

A fun dish all the family will enjoy. Have the cheesy nachos ready to pop under the grill as soon as the mince is cooked.

Serves 4

- 2 tbsp sunflower oil
- 1 onion, peeled and chopped
- 500 g (1 lb 2 oz) lean minced steak
- 2 tsp hot chilli powder
- 300 ml (½ pt) beef stock
- 400-g (14-oz) tin chopped tomatoes
- 2 tbsp sun-dried tomato purée
- 400-g (14-oz) tin red kidney beans, drained and rinsed

To serve

- Large bag nachos
- 100 g (4 oz) grated mature Cheddar cheese
- 1 avocado, stoned, peeled and chopped
- Soured cream

1 Heat the oil in a wok and fry the onion over a low heat until soft. Increase the heat to medium-high, add the minced steak, breaking up any clumps of meat with a wooden spoon, and fry until browned.

2 Add the chilli powder, fry for 1 minute and then add the stock, tomatoes and tomato purée. Simmer for 30 minutes.

3 Stir in the kidney beans and simmer for a further 10 minutes or until most of the liquid has evaporated and the sauce is thick and not too wet.

4 Meanwhile, spread out the nachos on a foil-lined grill rack and sprinkle with the cheese. Grill until the cheese melts.

5 Spoon the mince and beans into a serving dish and surround with the cheesy nachos and avocado. Serve with the soured cream to spoon over.

Kashmiri Lamb

**Warm and spicy with tender pieces of lamb and a sauce
thickened with creamy yogurt and ground almonds, this
makes a filling main course served with pilau rice (see
page 169), warm flatbreads or poppadums.**

Serves 4

- 2 tbsp vegetable oil
- 500 g (1 lb 2 oz) lean lamb, cubed
- 1 large red onion, peeled and sliced
- 1 sweet potato, peeled and cut into small chunks
- 3 tbsp curry paste (e.g. masala, rogan josh or jalfrezi)
- 50 g (2 oz) ground almonds
- 230-g (8-oz) tin chopped tomatoes
- 300 ml (½ pt) lamb stock
- 4 tbsp Greek-style natural yogurt
- Salt and freshly ground black pepper
- 4 tbsp chopped fresh coriander to serve

1 Heat the oil in a wok, add half the lamb and stir-fry over a high heat until sealed and browned. Remove and set aside. Add the rest of the lamb, brown and set aside.

2 Lower the heat, add the onion and sweet potato and fry for 5 minutes, stirring occasionally. Return the lamb to the wok and stir in the curry paste and ground almonds. Stir until the lamb and vegetables are coated, then add the tomatoes and stock.

3 Cover the wok with a lid and simmer gently for 45 minutes, or until the lamb is tender. Remove from the heat and stir in the yogurt 1 tablespoon at a time. Season to taste and reheat without boiling.

4 Serve sprinkled with the chopped coriander.

Use lamb cut from the shoulder or leg, trimming away any fat before cutting into cubes with a sharp knife.

Pork Spring Rolls with Water Chestnuts and Mushrooms

These make an unusual starter or light lunch dish served with sweet chilli sauce and a small salad garnish.

Serves 4

- 3 tbsp sunflower oil
- 100 g (4 oz) Chinese cabbage or pak choi, shredded
- ½ red pepper, deseeded and finely chopped
- 100 g (4 oz) shiitake mushrooms, finely chopped
- 3 spring onions, trimmed and chopped
- 4 tinned water chestnuts, finely chopped
- 1 garlic clove, peeled and crushed
- 1 tsp grated root ginger
- 1 red chilli, deseeded and very finely chopped
- 1 tbsp chopped fresh coriander
- 150 g (5 oz) lean pork steak, cut into very small dice
- 2 tbsp hoisin sauce
- 12 x 20-cm (7¾-in) spring roll wrappers
- 1 egg white, lightly beaten
- Soy sauce or sweet chilli sauce to serve

1 Heat 2 tablespoons of the oil in a wok and stir-fry the cabbage, red pepper, mushrooms, spring onions, water chestnuts, garlic, ginger and chilli over a medium heat for 5 minutes until softened. Sprinkle over the coriander, remove from the wok and transfer to a bowl.

2 Add the pork to the wok, stir-fry over a high heat for 4–5 minutes until browned. Stir in the plum or hoisin sauce until the pork is coated. Add to the bowl with the vegetables. Leave to cool.

3 Place a wrapper on a board and put a spoonful of the pork and vegetable mixture in the centre. Brush the edges of the wrapper with egg white, tuck in the sides and roll the wrapper around the filling, pressing the brushed edges together to seal it completely. Repeat with the remaining wrappers and filling.

4 Shallow-fry the rolls in batches in hot oil until golden all over. Drain on absorbent kitchen paper and serve hot with a dip of sweet chilli sauce.

Wrappers can be bought from Oriental food shops and are sold frozen in sealed packs, so they just need thawing and gently peeling apart.

Asian Pork Wraps

Pork mince simmered with aromatic Asian spices and then spooned on to crisp lettuce cups makes a colourful DIY dish – great to eat outdoors!

Serves 4

- 1 tbsp sunflower oil
- 2 garlic cloves, peeled and chopped
- 1 tsp grated root ginger or ginger purée
- 1 red chilli, deseeded and finely chopped
- 500 g (1 lb 2 oz) lean minced pork
- 2 tbsp Thai fish sauce
- 2 tbsp dark soy sauce
- 1 tbsp brown sugar
- Juice of 1 lime
- 250 ml (8 fl oz) chicken stock
- 1 tbsp chopped fresh mint
- 2 tbsp chopped fresh coriander

To serve
- Cup-shaped salad leaves
- 3 tbsp roasted, unsalted peanuts, chopped
- 1 red chilli, deseeded and cut into wafer-thin slices
- 2 spring onions, shredded

1 Heat the oil in a wok and cook the garlic, ginger and chilli over a medium heat for 1 minute.

2 Turn up the heat a little, add the pork mince and fry for 5–6 minutes or until the meat is browned, stirring frequently. Add the fish sauce, soy sauce, sugar, lime juice and stock and simmer for 15 minutes or until most of the excess liquid has evaporated and the sauce is quite thick. Stir in the mint and coriander.

3 To serve, separate the salad into individual leaves and divide between four serving plates. Leave diners to spoon a little meat mixture on to each leaf, top with peanuts, chilli slices and shredded spring onions and eat whole if the leaves are small or roll the leaves around the filling, if larger.

Use minced chicken or turkey if you prefer. If iceberg lettuce is used, remove the leaves without tearing them by holding the lettuce upright under cold slow running water and the leaves will peel away easily.

Teriyaki Steak with Spring Onions and Pak Choi

Serve this delicious sweet-sour dish on a bed of fine egg noodles. Teriyaki is Japanese soy sauce flavoured with mirin (sweet rice wine), sake and sugar and can be found amongst the Oriental ingredients in supermarkets.

Serves 4

- 500 g (1 lb 2 oz) rump or sirloin steak
- 4 tbsp teriyaki sauce
- Juice of 1 lime
- 1 tbsp sesame oil or 1 tsp toasted sesame oil
- 2 tbsp sunflower oil
- 4 spring onions, trimmed and cut into 2.5-cm (1-in) lengths
- 2 heads of pak choi, shredded
- 75 g (3 oz) bean sprouts

> **Toasted sesame oil has a much stronger, more concentrated flavour than ordinary sesame oil, so if you buy this, only add a very little or it will overpower the other ingredients.**

1 Trim any fat from the steak and cut the meat into thin strips across the grain. In a bowl, mix together the teriyaki sauce, lime juice and sesame oil and pour over the steak, turning the strips over until coated. Cover the dish with cling film and place in the fridge to marinate for 3–4 hours.

2 Heat the sunflower oil in a wok, lift half the steak from the marinade and stir-fry over a high heat for 2 minutes until browned. Remove from the wok and set aside. Add the rest of the steak to the wok, reserving the marinade, and stir-fry for 2 minutes.

3 Return the first batch of steak to the wok and add the spring onions, pak choi and bean sprouts. Stir-fry for 3 minutes, then pour over the marinade left in the dish and toss everything together over the heat for 1 minute, until piping hot. Serve immediately.

Cajun Hash Browns with Chorizo and Cherry Tomatoes

A great weekend brunch dish that is a good way of using up any potatoes you have left over from the night before. Instead of chorizo, you could also use Italian pepperoni or Moroccan merguez sausages.

Serves 4

- 700 g (1½ lb) waxy potatoes (e.g. Desirée)
- 2 tbsp sunflower oil
- 2 chorizo sausages, cut into bite-sized pieces
- 1 red pepper, deseeded and chopped
- 1 orange pepper, deseeded and chopped
- 6 spring onions, trimmed and chopped
- 75 g (3 oz) butter
- 1 tsp Cajun seasoning, or to taste
- 12 cherry tomatoes, halved
- 2 tbsp chopped fresh parsley

> **Fry the potatoes over a moderate heat so the butter doesn't brown too much and give the potatoes a burnt, bitter taste.**

1 Peel the potatoes and cut into even-sized chunks. Boil in a pan of water (you can use a wok for this as long as it is flat-bottomed or you have a wok burner) until just tender. Drain and coarsely crush or chop them into small pieces. (Carefully dry the wok if you have used it to boil the potatoes.)

2 Heat the oil in the wok, add the chorizo pieces and fry for 5 minutes over a medium heat. Add the peppers and spring onions and fry for a further 5 minutes. Remove from the wok and set aside.

3 Add the butter to the wok and, when melted, tip in the potatoes and sprinkle over the Cajun seasoning. Fry for 10 minutes until golden brown, stirring and turning the pieces over occasionally. Stir in the chorizo, peppers, spring onions and cherry tomato halves. Fry for a further 5 minutes until the potatoes are crisp and the chorizo and vegetables are piping hot. Sprinkle with the parsley and serve.

Marinated Steak in Tomato and Wild Mushroom Sauce

New potatoes are an irresistible accompaniment to these steaks, with a salad of mixed leaves to lessen the guilt. Trim fat from the steaks before marinating them, which tenderizes the meat as well as adding aroma and flavour.

Serves 4

- 4 sirloin or rump steaks
- 2 garlic cloves, peeled and finely chopped
- 150 ml (¼ pt) red wine
- 6 tbsp olive oil
- Juice of ½ lemon
- Freshly ground black pepper
- 1 large onion, peeled and finely chopped
- 150 g (5 oz) mixed mushrooms, chopped
- 500 g (1 lb 2 oz) ripe tomatoes, skinned, deseeded and chopped
- 2 tbsp chopped fresh parsley

1 Lay the steaks in a shallow dish in a single layer. Mix together the garlic, red wine, 2 tablespoons of the olive oil and the lemon juice and season with plenty of freshly ground black pepper. Pour over the steaks, cover with cling film and leave in the fridge to marinate for several hours or overnight.

2 Put 2 tablespoons of the olive oil in a wok and, over a low heat, sauté the onion and mushrooms for 5 minutes. Lift the steaks from the marinade and set aside. Add the marinade to the wok with the tomatoes and simmer for 25–30 minutes until excess liquid has evaporated and the sauce is thick. Pour the sauce into a heatproof dish and keep warm in a low oven.

3 Carefully rinse the wok and wipe clean with absorbent kitchen paper. Heat the rest of the oil in the wok and fry the steaks over a high heat until browned on both sides. Lower the heat and continue to cook until done to your liking.

4 Serve the steaks with the sauce spooned over, sprinkled with chopped parsley.

If ripe, flavoursome tomatoes aren't in season, use a 400-g (14-oz) tin of chopped tomatoes instead.

Creamy Pork with Mushrooms and Peppers

A colourful one-pot family supper that's perfect for cooking in a wok. The pork can be served on its own with hunks of warm sourdough or ciabatta or accompanied by boiled rice or new potatoes.

Serves 4

- 2 tbsp sunflower oil
- 500 g (1 lb 2 oz) pork steaks, cut into thin strips
- 1 large onion, peeled and thinly sliced
- 1 garlic clove, peeled and crushed
- 175 g (6 oz) mushrooms, sliced or quartered
- 1 red pepper, deseeded and sliced
- 1 orange or yellow pepper, deseeded and sliced
- 1 tbsp tomato purée
- 2 tbsp peanut butter (smooth or crunchy)
- 150 ml (¼ pt) chicken stock
- 200 ml (7 fl oz) crème fraîche or double cream
- Salt and freshly ground black pepper
- 2 tbsp snipped fresh chives

1 Heat 1 tablespoon of the oil in a wok and stir-fry the pork in two batches over a brisk heat for 5 minutes each batch or until the strips are lightly browned. Drain from the wok and set aside.

2 Add the rest of the oil to the wok, lower the heat and add the onion. Cover and fry for 5 minutes until starting to soften, then remove the lid and add the garlic, mushrooms and peppers. Increase the heat to medium and fry the vegetables for 5 minutes, stirring frequently.

3 Add the tomato purée and peanut butter, return the pork and any juices from it to the wok and stir in the stock. Bring to the boil, then lower the heat and simmer for 5 minutes.

4 Stir in the crème fraîche or double cream and season to taste. Simmer for a further 2 minutes, sprinkle with the chives and serve immediately.

If you're counting the calories, low-fat crème fraîche, single cream or natural yogurt can be used instead of full-fat varieties, but stir them in a spoonful at a time and don't let the sauce boil or it will separate. Alternatively, mix low-fat cream or yogurt with 1 teaspoon of cornflour and stir the sauce as it comes to the boil.

Lamb, Spinach and Aubergine Curry

Ready-prepared spice mixes take the strain out of curry making. The mixes vary in strength, so choose one that suits your taste buds – korma or masala for a mild flavour, jalfrezi, Madras or vindaloo if you like it hot.

Serves 4

- 4 tbsp vegetable or sunflower oil
- 500 g (1 lb 2 oz) lean lamb, diced
- 2 medium onions, peeled and chopped
- 1 aubergine, cut into 1-cm (½-in) cubes
- 1 red pepper, deseeded and chopped
- 2 mild green chillies, deseeded and finely chopped
- 2 garlic cloves, peeled and finely chopped
- 2 tbsp curry paste
- 1 tsp paprika
- 400-g (14-oz) tin chopped tomatoes
- 300 ml (½ pt) lamb stock
- 175 g (6 oz) spinach leaves, shredded
- 4 tbsp chopped fresh coriander

1 Heat half the oil in a wok and brown the lamb in batches over a fairly high heat. Remove the pieces with a slotted spoon as they brown and set aside.

2 Add the rest of the oil to the wok and lower the heat. Fry the onions for 10 minutes until softened, then add the aubergine, red pepper, chillies and garlic and fry for a further 5 minutes.

3 Stir in the curry paste, paprika, tomatoes and stock and bring to a simmer. Return the lamb to the wok, cover and simmer gently for 45 minutes, stirring occasionally. Stir in the shredded spinach and cook for 2–3 minutes until the leaves wilt.

4 Serve the curry sprinkled with the coriander, with boiled rice and poppadums or naan bread.

Lamb cut from the leg or shoulder joint is best for this curry. Trim away any fat or sinew before dicing the meat. Curry powder could be used instead of paste but fry it off in the wok with the aubergine and red pepper before adding the tomatoes and stock.

Stir-fried Pork with Cashews and Spinach

Lean strips of pork stir-fried with colourful vegetables and crunchy cashews makes a tasty lunch or supper for two. It's not essential to marinate the meat, but if you have time – even for just an hour or so – it will be much more flavourful.

Serves 2

- 250 g (9 oz) lean pork steaks, cut into thin strips
- 2 tbsp hoisin sauce
- 2 tbsp dark soy sauce
- 1 tsp ground coriander
- 1 tsp grated root ginger or ginger purée
- 2 tbsp sunflower oil
- 50 g (2 oz) unsalted cashews
- 1 carrot, peeled and cut into julienne
- 4 spring onions, cut into short lengths
- 150 g (5 oz) mushrooms, quartered or sliced
- 75 g (3 oz) spinach leaves, shredded

1 Place the pork strips in a shallow dish. Mix together the hoisin sauce, soy sauce, ground coriander and ginger and spoon over the pork, turning the strips over until they are well coated. Cover and leave in the fridge for several hours or overnight.

2 Heat 1 tablespoon of the oil in a wok, add the cashews and stir-fry for about 30 seconds until golden. Drain from the wok and set aside.

3 Add the carrot, spring onions and mushrooms to the pan and stir-fry over a high heat for 3 minutes. Remove from the wok and set aside.

4 Add the rest of the oil to the wok, lift the pork from the marinade and stir-fry for 3 minutes. Return the carrot, spring onions, mushrooms and cashews to the wok and pour in any marinade left in the dish. Add the spinach and stir-fry for 2 minutes until the spinach has wilted.

Serve the pork with Egg Fried Rice with Bacon, Peppers and Peas (see page 144), plain boiled rice or Chinese egg noodles.

Sizzling Black Bean Beef

Stir-fries are always satisfying dishes to cook as the ingredients seal quickly in the pan and everything retains all its colour and flavour. Use other vegetables if you prefer, the ones listed below are only suggestions.

Serves 2

- 2 tbsp groundnut oil
- 2 shallots or baby onions, peeled and thinly sliced
- ½ orange pepper, deseeded and chopped
- 150 g (5 oz) tenderstem broccoli
- 100 g (4 oz) mushrooms, quartered
- 100 g (4 oz) dried vermicelli rice noodles
- 350 g (12 oz) rump or sirloin steak, cut into thin strips
- 1 jar or sachet (about 175 g/6 oz) black bean stir-fry sauce
- 1 red chilli, deseeded and sliced

1 Heat the oil in a wok and stir-fry the shallots, orange pepper and tenderstem broccoli over a high heat for 3 minutes. Add the mushrooms and stir-fry for a further 3 minutes.

2 Meanwhile, place the rice noodles in a bowl and cover them with boiling water. Set aside for 4 minutes.

3 Remove the vegetables from the pan and set aside. Keep the heat high and add the steak. Stir-fry for 2 minutes. Stir in the black bean sauce.

4 Drain the noodles thoroughly and add to the pan with the vegetables. Toss everything together over the heat for 1–2 minutes or until the steak, noodles and vegetables are piping hot.

5 Serve immediately with the chilli sprinkled over.

This could be made with pork, lamb or chicken, but always slice the meat across the grain so the fibres running down it are short, thus ensuring it stays tender when cooked.

Sherry-braised Pork with Mushrooms and Chorizo

Full-flavoured and deeply satisfying, this Spanish-inspired dish needs little accompaniment beyond new potatoes or boiled rice.

Serves 4

- 2 tbsp sunflower oil
- 500 g (1 lb 2 oz) lean pork, cut into bite-sized pieces
- 175 g (6 oz) chorizo, cut into bite-sized pieces
- 8 baby onions, peeled
- 12 baby carrots, scrubbed and halved lengthways
- 100 ml (3½ fl oz) dry sherry
- 2 tsp cornflour
- 450 ml (¾ pt) chicken stock
- 2 tbsp tomato purée
- 1 tbsp brown sugar
- 100 g (4 oz) button mushrooms
- Juice of 1 lime
- 2 tbsp chopped fresh tarragon
- 2 tomatoes, skinned and chopped
- Freshly ground black pepper

1 Heat half the oil in a wok and stir-fry the pork and chorizo in batches over a high heat until browned. Remove from the wok and set aside.

2 Add the rest of the oil to the wok, lower the heat and fry the onions and carrots for 5 minutes until the onions start to brown. Pour in the sherry and leave to bubble for 1 minute.

3 Mix the cornflour with a little of the stock until smooth and add to the wok with the rest of the stock, tomato purée, sugar, mushrooms, lime juice and half the tarragon.

4 Stir until the sauce thickens, return the pork and chorizo to the wok, add the tomatoes and cover with a lid. Simmer gently for 30 minutes.

5 Season with freshly ground black pepper and sprinkle with the rest of the tarragon.

Instead of chorizo try substituting the spicy Moroccan sausage, merguez. Allow 1 merguez per person and twist them into short lengths measuring about 4cm (1½ in) before adding them to the wok.

Lamb in Sticky Barbecue Sauce

Mustard and Worcestershire sauce give this stir-fried lamb a subtle spicy kick, while brown sugar and tomato ketchup add a touch of sweetness. Prepare the lamb well ahead so it has plenty of time to absorb the flavours of the marinade.

Serves 4

- 500 g (1 lb 2 oz) lean lamb, cut into strips
- 2 garlic cloves, peeled and finely chopped
- 2 tbsp light brown sugar
- 2 tsp Dijon mustard
- 3 tbsp sun-dried tomato purée
- 2 tbsp vinegar
- 2 tbsp tomato ketchup
- 1 tsp Worcestershire sauce
- 3 tbsp vegetable oil
- 1 onion, peeled and finely chopped
- 100 g (4 oz) mushrooms, sliced
- 1 red pepper, deseeded and sliced
- 150 ml (¼ pt) apple juice
- 1 tsp cornflour

1 Spread out the lamb in a shallow dish. Whisk together the garlic, sugar, mustard, tomato purée, vinegar, ketchup and Worcestershire sauce, whisking until the sugar dissolves. Pour over the lamb, turning the strips until coated. Cover and leave in the fridge to marinate for 3–4 hours or overnight.

2 Heat 1 tablespoon of the oil in a wok and stir-fry the onion, mushrooms and pepper over a high heat for 3 minutes. Drain and set aside.

3 Add the rest of the oil to the wok, lift half the lamb from the marinade and stir-fry over a high heat for 3–4 minutes until browned. Drain and set aside. Repeat with the rest of the lamb.

4 Mix the apple juice and cornflour together until blended and pour into the wok with the marinade left in the dish. Stir over the heat until bubbling, then return the vegetables and lamb to the wok and stir everything together for 1–2 minutes until heated through. Serve immediately with rice, or new potatoes and a green vegetable.

> **Strips of pork or rump steak could be used instead of lamb and, for a more substantial dish, stir in a 400-g (14-oz) tin of baked beans in tomato sauce or a well-drained 400-g (14-oz) tin of kidney beans and a 225-g (8-oz) tin of chopped tomatoes.**

GRAINS, NOODLES,
RICE AND PULSES

Garlic Chicken and Vegetable Rice

Chicken and vegetables quickly stir-fried in the wok then mixed with basmati rice and flavoured with garlic, ginger and soy sauce, makes a simple one-pot meal. Vary the selection of vegetables according to what you have available.

Serves 4

- 500 g (1 lb 2 oz) boneless, skinless chicken breasts, diced
- 1 tbsp cornflour
- 3 tbsp vegetable oil
- 2 large garlic cloves, peeled and left whole
- 4 spring onions, trimmed and sliced
- 175 g (6 oz) tenderstem broccoli
- 150 g (5 oz) shiitake mushrooms, sliced
- 100 g (4 oz) baby corn, halved
- 1 tsp grated root ginger or ginger purée
- 2 tbsp light soy sauce
- 225 g (8 oz) freshly-cooked basmati rice

1 Toss the diced chicken with the cornflour until coated. Heat 2 tablespoons of the oil in a wok and fry the garlic over a low heat until golden brown. Drain and discard the garlic cloves.

2 Turn up the heat to medium-high, add half the chicken and stir-fry for 5 minutes or until lightly browned. Remove and set aside. Repeat with the rest of the chicken.

3 Add the remaining oil and stir-fry the spring onions and broccoli over a high heat for 2 minutes. Add the mushrooms, baby corn and ginger and stir-fry for 3 minutes.

3 Add the soy sauce, return the chicken to the wok and stir in the rice. Toss everything together for 2–3 minutes until heated through. Serve immediately.

Wild Mushroom and Parmesan Risotto

A good risotto takes time and patience to make, but the end result is well worth the effort involved. Full-flavoured mushrooms, aromatic fresh herbs and tangy Parmesan contrast perfectly with the creamy rice.

Serves 4

- 5 tbsp olive oil
- 500 g (1 lb 2 oz) mixed mushrooms (e.g. chestnut, shiitake, oyster, porcini) sliced or quartered according to size
- 1 onion, peeled and finely sliced
- 2 garlic cloves, peeled and crushed
- 2 tsp chopped fresh oregano
- Finely grated zest of ½ lemon
- 350 g (12 oz) Arborio rice
- 150 ml (¼ pt) dry white wine
- 900 ml (1½ pt) hot chicken or vegetable stock
- 3 tbsp grated Parmesan, plus extra for shavings
- 2 tbsp snipped fresh chives
- Freshly ground black pepper

1 Heat 3 tablespoons of the oil in a wok and stir-fry the mushrooms over a medium heat for 5 minutes. Drain and set aside.

2 Add the rest of the oil to the wok, lower the heat and fry the onion and garlic for 5 minutes. Add the oregano, lemon zest and rice, stirring for 1–2 minutes until the grains are shiny.

3 Pour in the wine, bring to the boil and leave to bubble until the wine has nearly all evaporated. Add a ladleful of the hot stock and stir until it has been absorbed by the rice. Continue adding the stock, a ladleful at a time, allowing each lot to be absorbed before adding the next, until the rice is tender – this will take around 20 minutes.

4 Stir in the grated Parmesan and then the mushrooms into the rice and scatter over the chives. Season with freshly ground black pepper and serve with Parmesan shavings scattered on top..

Risotto should be moist and creamy when it is cooked, not dry like a pilaf, so add extra stock if necessary.

Chicken, Mangetout and Vermicelli Soup

A Chinese broth that's often dubbed 'long soup' as long vermicelli noodles are added to it, rather than 'short' wontons. Cubes or powder can be used to make the stock or make your own – but season it well or the soup will taste bland.

Serves 4

- 40 g (1½ oz) dried Chinese mushrooms
- 600 ml (1 pt) well-flavoured chicken stock
- 175 g (6 oz) dried rice vermicelli
- 2 boneless, skinless chicken breasts, cut into very thin strips
- 150 g (5 oz) mangetout, cut into very thin strips

1 Put the mushrooms in a heatproof jug or bowl and pour over 300 ml (½ pt) boiling water. Leave for 30 minutes. Strain the soaking liquid into a wok and add the stock. Slice the mushrooms into long thin strips.

2 Break or snip the rice vermicelli into short lengths with kitchen scissors, stir into the stock and bring to a simmer. Cook for 2 minutes, then add the chicken strips and mushrooms. Simmer for a further 2 minutes.

3 Add the mangetout and simmer for 1 minute until the mangetout are heated through but they remain a little crisp.

4 Spoon into warmed bowls and serve immediately.

To make the soup more substantial, add extra vegetables such as sweetcorn, finely chopped green pepper or peas and replace the rice vermicelli with thicker noodles, such as flat rice noodles or medium egg noodles.

Stir-fried Pork with Crispy Noodles

Rice vermicelli, flash-fried until crisp, makes an unusual accompaniment to the spicy pork and cashews. Cook the noodles first and keep them warm in a low oven, uncovered, while you stir-fry the meat.

Serves 4

- Vegetable oil for frying
- 150 g (5 oz) dried rice vermicelli
- 1 green pepper, deseeded and chopped
- 150 g (5 oz) mushrooms, sliced, or whole if small
- 8 spring onions, trimmed and sliced
- 500 g (1 lb 2 oz) lean pork steaks, cubed
- 3 tbsp dark soy sauce
- 2 tbsp oyster sauce
- 2 tsp Thai green curry paste
- 1 tsp light brown sugar
- 2 tbsp natural roasted peanuts, chopped

1 Heat about 5 cm (2 in) vegetable oil in a wok to 190°C (375°F) or until a cube of bread browns in 30 seconds.

2 Snip the vermicelli into short lengths and deep-fry in small batches for a few seconds until they puff up and turn white and crisp. Drain and keep them warm in a low oven – don't cover them or they will go soggy.

3 When they have all been fried, tip all but 2 tablespoons of the oil into a heatproof bowl and leave in a safe place to cool. Wipe any drips off the outside of the wok and place over a medium-high heat.

4 Add the pepper, mushrooms and spring onions and stir-fry for 5 minutes. Remove and set aside.

5 Turn up the heat to high, add the pork and stir-fry for 3 minutes until the meat is browned. Mix together the soy sauce,

oyster sauce, green curry paste and sugar and pour over the meat, tossing until coated. Return the vegetables to the wok, sprinkle over the peanuts and stir-fry for 1 minute.

6 Divide the noodles between serving plates and pile the pork and vegetables on top. Serve immediately.

It's important to heat the oil to the correct temperature, otherwise the noodles will be tough and chewy instead of light and crisp.

Spicy Moroccan Chicken Couscous

Exotic aromas of a kasbah spice market flavour this colourful chicken dish, which mixes dried apricots, toasted cashews and black olives with golden grains of cous cous.

Serves 4

- 225 g (8 oz) couscous
- Pinch of saffron strands
- 1 tbsp sunflower oil
- 2 shallots, peeled and chopped
- ½ red pepper, deseeded and chopped
- 1 tbsp ground coriander
- 1 tsp ground cumin
- 1 tsp harissa paste
- 500 g (1 lb 2 oz) boneless, skinless chicken breasts, cubed
- 50 g (2 oz) dried apricots, chopped
- 50 g (2 oz) toasted, unsalted cashews
- 12 black olives

Dressing

- 6 tbsp natural yogurt
- 1 tbsp sunflower oil
- 1 tbsp lemon juice
- 2 tbsp chopped fresh mint
- Paprika, to dust

1 Place the couscous in a large heatproof bowl, crumble over the saffron strands and pour boiling water over to cover. Leave to stand for 10 minutes or until the grains have swollen and absorbed the water.

2 Meanwhile, heat the oil in a wok and fry the shallots and red pepper over a low heat for 5 minutes. Add the coriander, cumin and harissa and cook for 2 minutes.

3 Increase the heat to medium. Add the chicken and cook for 5 minutes, stirring occasionally. Drain any surplus water from the couscous and add to the wok with the apricots, cashews and olives. Stir over the heat for 3 minutes or until everything is piping hot.

4 To make the dressing, whisk the yogurt, oil and lemon juice together in a small bowl. Stir in the mint, dust with paprika and serve with the chicken couscous.

Harissa is a hot chilli paste often used to spice up North African dishes. Find it in larger supermarkets among the spices or substitute with hot chilli sauce.

Lamb, Almond and Saffron Pilaf

A great supper dish that needs little to accompany it except perhaps a leafy green salad.

Serves 4

- 4 tbsp sunflower oil
- 350 g (12 oz) lean lamb, cut into 1-cm (½-in) cubes
- 2 onions, peeled and chopped
- 1 aubergine, chopped
- 2 tsp ground coriander
- 400-g (14-oz) tin chopped tomatoes
- 225 g (8 oz) basmati rice
- 350 ml (12 fl oz) lamb stock
- Few saffron strands soaked in 2 tbsp hot (previously boiled) water for 5 minutes
- 50 g (2 oz) toasted flaked almonds
- 2 tbsp chopped fresh parsley

Leave the pilaf to stand for 10 minutes before serving: the rice will finish cooking in its own steam,

1 Heat 2 tablespoons of the oil in a wok and brown the lamb in batches by stir-frying over a high heat. As the lamb cubes brown, remove them to a plate and set aside.

2 Lower the heat, add the rest of the oil to the wok and fry the onions until softened. Add the aubergine and coriander and cook for 3 minutes, stirring occasionally.

3 Stir in the tomatoes, return the lamb to the wok, put the lid on and simmer gently for 40 minutes.

4 Stir in the rice, stock, saffron and its soaking water and bring to the boil. Cover and simmer for 20 minutes then remove from the heat and, with the lid still on, leave to stand for 10 minutes.

5 Fork up the rice and serve with the almonds and chopped parsley sprinkled over.

Chicken and Seafood Laksa

A dish that's often eaten as a snack in the Malay Peninsula, laksa takes its name from a dark green leaf, also known as Vietnamese mint, which is used to flavour the dish in Asia. Here the mint is replaced by more readily-available coriander.

Serves 4

- 3 tbsp vegetable oil
- 175 g (6 oz) mangetout, sliced
- 100 g (4 oz) bean sprouts
- 4 shallots, peeled and sliced
- 2 garlic cloves, peeled and crushed
- 1 tsp lemon grass purée
- ½ tsp shrimp paste
- 2 red chillies, deseeded and finely chopped
- 600 ml (1 pt) chicken stock
- 400 ml (14 fl oz) coconut milk
- 1 tbsp soft brown sugar
- 2 skinless boneless chicken breasts, cut into 2-cm (1-in) pieces
- 300 g (10 oz) raw tiger prawns, peeled
- 100 g (4 oz) dried mung bean noodles
- Fresh coriander leaves
- 2 spring onions, shredded

1 Heat 1 tablespoon of the oil in a wok and stir-fry the mangetout and bean sprouts over a high heat for 2–3 minutes until starting to soften. Remove from the wok, set aside and keep warm.

2 Add the rest of the oil to the wok, lower the heat and fry the shallots until softened. Add the garlic, lemon grass purée, shrimp paste and chillies and cook gently for 3 minutes. Stir in the stock, coconut milk and sugar, bring to a simmer and add the chicken and prawns. Cook gently for 5 minutes, or until the chicken is done.

3 While the soup is cooking, soak the noodles for 3–4 minutes in boiling water or according to the packet instructions. Drain and divide between serving bowls. Spoon the mangetout and bean sprouts on top and ladle in the hot soup.

4 Serve garnished with fresh coriander leaves and shredded spring onions.

133

Pad Thai with Shredded Omelette

Probably Thailand's most popular dish, after its famous red and green curries. The chopped roasted peanuts scattered over the spicy mix of chicken, prawns and noodles add a pleasing crunch to the finished dish.

Serves 4

- 350 g (12 oz) dried medium flat rice stick noodles
- 2 tbsp vegetable oil
- 4 large eggs
- 4 shallots, peeled and sliced
- 1 boneless, skinless chicken breast, cut into small chunks
- 200 g (7 oz) raw tiger prawns, peeled
- 1 tbsp oyster sauce
- 2 tbsp Thai fish sauce
- Juice of 1 lime
- 1 tsp brown sugar
- 225 g (8 oz) bean sprouts
- 4 spring onions, shredded
- 100 g (4 oz) natural roasted peanuts, roughly chopped
- 1 red chilli, deseeded and finely chopped
- 2 tbsp chopped fresh coriander

1 Cook the rice noodles according to the packet instructions, then drain and set aside.

2 Heat 1 tablespoon of the oil in a wok. Beat one of the eggs and pour into the wok, tilting the pan so the egg spreads out in a very thin layer. Cook until the underneath has set, then flip it over to cook the other side. Slide the omelette out of the pan on to a plate and keep warm in a low oven.

3 Add the rest of the oil to the wok and stir-fry the shallots and chicken over a fairly high heat for 2 minutes. Add the prawns and stir-fry for 1 minute.

4 Beat the remaining eggs, pour into the pan and stir until the eggs scramble. Add the oyster sauce, fish sauce, lime juice, sugar and noodles and stir-fry for 2 minutes.

5 Add the bean sprouts, spring onions and half the peanuts and toss everything together over the heat until piping hot.

6 Transfer to serving plates and scatter over the remaining peanuts. Roll up the omelette, slice thinly and scatter over the noodles with the chilli and coriander.

Popular with Vietnamese and Thai cooks, rice stick noodles look very much like rice vermicelli but are slightly broader and thicker. They can range from fine to medium in width, the latter resembling white fettucine.

Chicken and Shiitake Mushroom Chow Mein

A great Chinese favourite that can be served as a simple supper or as part of a larger spread. Use whatever vegetables you have available, but go for contrasting flavours and textures to add extra interest to the finished dish.

Serves 4

- 4 tbsp vegetable oil
- 1 red onion, peeled and thinly sliced
- 2 tsp grated root ginger or ginger purée
- 150 g (5 oz) shiitake mushrooms, quartered or sliced
- 1 red pepper, deseeded and thinly sliced
- 3 boneless, skinless chicken breasts, cut into bite-sized pieces
- 100 g (4 oz) mangetout, sliced in half lengthways
- 100 g (4 oz) bean sprouts
- 350 g (12 oz) fresh medium wheatflour noodles
- 4 tbsp dark soy sauce, plus extra for sprinkling
- 1 tbsp rice wine or dry sherry
- 100 ml (3½ fl oz) chicken stock
- 1 tsp cornflour

1 Heat 2 tablespoons of the oil in a wok and stir-fry the onion, ginger, mushrooms and red pepper over a medium-high heat for 5 minutes. Remove and set aside.

2 Turn up the heat to high, add the remaining oil and stir-fry half the chicken for 3 minutes. Remove, add the rest of the chicken to the wok and stir-fry for 3 minutes. Remove and set aside.

3 Add the mangetout and bean sprouts, lower the heat to medium-high and stir-fry for 2 minutes. Add the noodles, then return the chicken and vegetables to the wok.

4 Mix together 4 tablespoons of the soy sauce, the wine or sherry, stock and cornflour until smooth and pour into the wok. Toss everything together over the heat for 2 minutes until piping hot. Serve with extra soy sauce to sprinkle over.

If fresh noodles are not available, use 175 g (6 oz) dried and cook them according to the packet instructions before you begin stir-frying.

Devilled Chicken and Prawn Jambalaya

Packed with spicy flavours, this favourite dish from America's Deep South has everything you need in one pot. It's equally good for a family supper or if you have friends dropping by for dinner.

Serves 4

- 2 tbsp vegetable oil
- 350 g (12 oz) boneless, skinless chicken breasts, cut into small pieces
- 150 g (5 oz) chorizo sausage, cut into small pieces
- 1 tsp Cajun seasoning
- 1 onion, peeled and sliced
- 1 celery stick, sliced
- 1 green pepper, deseeded and chopped
- 2 garlic cloves, peeled and crushed
- 1 jalapeno chilli, deseeded and finely chopped
- 225 g (8 oz) long-grain rice
- 6 tbsp creole sauce or spicy tomato sauce
- 750 ml (1¼ pt) hot chicken stock
- 200 g (7 oz) cooked, peeled prawns
- 2 tbsp fresh chopped coriander

1 Heat 1 tablespoon of the oil in a wok, add the chicken, chorizo and Cajun seasoning and stir-fry over a high heat for 3 minutes. Remove from the wok, lower the heat and add the onion, celery, green pepper, garlic and chilli and fry for 5 minutes.

2 Stir in the rice, return the chicken and chorizo to the wok. Stir in the creole sauce and about three-quarters of the stock, and bring to the boil.

3 Simmer gently for 15–20 minutes or until the rice is cooked, adding more stock as needed to stop the mixture becoming too dry and sticking to the wok before it is ready. Stir in the prawns and coriander, heat through for 2–3 minutes and serve.

The creole sauce can be found among the Mexican ingredients on supermarket shelves and is a chunky mix of tomatoes and peppers. It might also be labelled taco or burrito sauce, but if you have trouble finding it, Italian arabbiata sauce is a good substitute.

Lemon Dhal with Onions and Leeks

A wholesome lentil dish that can be eaten on its own or to accompany other meat or fish curries. A few mustard seeds scattered over the top give the lentils a fiery kick.

Serves 4

- 2 tbsp vegetable oil
- 2 red onions, peeled and thinly sliced
- 2 onions, peeled and thinly sliced
- 1 leek, trimmed and thinly sliced
- 2 garlic cloves, peeled and crushed
- 1 tsp grated root ginger
- 1 green chilli, deseeded and finely chopped
- 1 tbsp curry paste
- 200 g (7 oz) yellow or red lentils
- ½ tsp turmeric
- 230-g (8-oz) tin chopped tomatoes
- Grated zest and juice of 1 lemon
- 2 tbsp chopped fresh coriander
- 1 tsp black mustard seeds (optional)

1 Heat the oil in a wok and fry the onions, leek and garlic over a low heat until soft and golden. Stir in the ginger, chilli and curry paste and fry for 1 minute, then remove from the wok and set aside.

2 Pour 600 ml (1 pt) water into the wok and bring to the boil. Stir in the lentils and turmeric, bring back to the boil, cover the wok with a lid and simmer gently for 20 minutes or until the lentils are soft and they have absorbed the water.

3 Stir the tomatoes and lemon juice into the lentils with the fried onion and leek mixture and simmer for 5 minutes.

4 Serve sprinkled with the grated lemon zest, chopped coriander and mustard seeds.

The dhal can be cooked in advance and reheated gently until piping hot.
Give the lentil mixture a good stir before reheating.

Chicken with Red Rice and Black-eyed Beans

Wild rice adds a deliciously nutty flavour, while the potatoes and orange juice give a hint of sweetness. This could easily be adapted for vegetarians by replacing the chicken with green beans, carrots and red pepper, and using vegetable stock.

Serves 4

- 2 tbsp olive oil
- 4 boneless, skinless chicken breasts or 8 chicken thighs, cut into chunks
- 1 leek, sliced
- 2 small sweet potatoes, peeled and cut into 2-cm (¾-in) chunks
- 1 courgette, sliced
- 100 g (4 oz) button mushrooms, halved
- 225 g (8 oz) mixed long-grain and wild rice
- 400-g (14-oz) tin chopped tomatoes
- 450 ml (¾ pt) chicken stock
- 150 ml (¼ pt) fresh orange juice
- 410-g (14-½ oz) tin black-eyed beans, drained and rinsed

1 Heat the oil in a wok and brown the chicken in batches over a high heat. Remove the chicken from the wok and set aside.

2 Lower the heat under the wok, add the leek, sweet potatoes, courgette and mushrooms and fry for 10 minutes, stirring frequently.

3 Stir in the rice, then add the tomatoes, stock and orange juice. Bring to a simmer, return the chicken to the wok, add the beans and bring to the boil.

4 Simmer gently for 20 minutes or until the rice and sweet potatoes are tender, stirring towards the end of the cooking time to prevent the rice from sticking.

Egg Fried Rice with Bacon, Peppers and Peas

A classic Chinese favourite that makes an excellent family supper or relaxed meal for friends. Ring the changes by adding whatever vegetables you have available, but chop them into small similar-sized pieces so they cook evenly.

Serves 4

- 2 tbsp vegetable oil
- 4 rashers of lean back bacon, chopped
- ½ red pepper, deseeded and finely chopped
- ½ orange pepper, deseeded and finely chopped
- 100 g (4 oz) button mushrooms, halved or quartered
- 1 tsp Chinese five spice powder
- 1 tsp dried chilli flakes
- 100 g (4 oz) frozen peas
- 3 spring onions, finely chopped
- 2 large eggs, beaten
- 225 g (8 oz) freshly-cooked long-grain rice
- 2 tbsp light soy sauce
- 3 spring onions, finely sliced lengthways

1 Heat the oil in a wok and stir-fry the bacon over a high heat for 2 minutes. Add the peppers, stir-fry for 3 minutes, then add the mushrooms and stir-fry for 2 minutes.

2 Lower the heat to medium, add the five spice powder, chilli, frozen peas and the chopped onions and stir-fry for 2 minutes.

3 Push everything to one side of the wok, pour in the eggs and leave until they start to set, then scramble with a fork. Mix with the bacon and vegetables, add the rice and soy sauce and toss everything together over the heat for 2 minutes.

4 Spoon the rice into serving bowls and pile the sliced spring onions on top.

> **It's not necessary to thaw the peas before you add them to the wok, as they'll soon defrost with the other ingredients which are hot.**

Stir-fried Soba with Shredded Chicken

Japanese Soba noodles are made from buckwheat flour and ordinary wheat flour and are traditionally eaten in Japan at midnight on New Year's Eve to bring diners luck and good health during the coming year.

Serves 4

- 225 g (8 oz) dried soba noodles
- 3 tbsp groundnut oil
- 2 boneless, skinless chicken breasts, cut into thin strips
- 1 onion, peeled and finely sliced
- 2 garlic cloves, peeled and crushed
- 1 tbsp pink pickled ginger, finely chopped
- 1 red pepper, deseeded and thinly sliced
- 100 g (4 oz) sugar snap peas, sliced lengthways
- 175 g (6 oz) Chinese cabbage leaves, shredded
- 2 tbsp mirin
- 2 tbsp rice vinegar
- 4 tbsp Japanese soy sauce
- 1 tsp toasted sesame oil

1 Cook the noodles in a large pan of boiling water according to the packet instructions until tender and then drain. This can be done in a wok or in a separate saucepan as you prefer.

2 Carefully dry the wok, if necessary, add 2 tablespoons of the groundnut oil and stir-fry the chicken over a high heat for 3–4 minutes until browned. Drain and set aside.

3 Add the remaining groundnut oil to the wok and stir-fry the onion, garlic and ginger for 3 minutes or until softened. Add the red pepper and sugar snap peas and stir-fry for 3 minutes.

4 Add the shredded cabbage and stir-fry for 2 minutes. Return the chicken and noodles to the wok and add the mirin, rice vinegar, soy sauce and sesame oil. Toss everything together for 2 minutes until heated through and serve at once.

Pink pickled ginger has a mild flavour and is usually served as an accompaniment to sushi and sashimi, while mirin is a sweet rice wine used for cooking in Japan. Both can be found in larger supermarkets and Oriental food stores.

Chicken and Spinach Pot with Udon

Thick udon noodles are used to make this hearty soup that is a main meal in a bowl. Chop the noodles into shorter lengths after cooking so diners don't have trouble scooping them up in their soup spoons!

Serves 4

- 2 boneless, skinless chicken breasts, cut into small cubes
- 2 tbsp Japanese soy sauce
- 1 tbsp rice vinegar
- 350 g (12 oz) dried thick udon noodles
- 750 ml (1¼ pt) chicken stock
- 1 carrot, peeled and cut into julienne
- 100 g (4 oz) shiitake mushrooms, thinly sliced
- 4 spring onions, thinly sliced
- 175 g (6 oz) spinach leaves, shredded

> **Udon are white wheat noodles from Japan that are available in different thicknesses. Widely used for soups and stews, they can be bought dried or fresh from Asian food stores.**

1 Put the chicken, soy sauce and rice vinegar in a dish and leave to marinate in the fridge for 30 minutes.

2 Cook the noodles in a pan of boiling water according to the packet instructions until just tender, then drain and snip into short lengths with kitchen scissors. Keep warm. You can cook the noodles either in the wok or another pan.

3 Pour the stock into the wok, add the carrot and mushrooms and bring to a simmer. Cook for 3 minutes, then add the chicken and its marinade, bring to the boil and simmer for 5 minutes.

4 Add the spring onions and spinach and simmer for 1–2 minutes or until the spinach has wilted.

5 Divide the noodles between four serving bowls and spoon over the hot soup. Serve immediately.

Thai Red Seafood with Rice Stick Noodles

Bite-sized pieces of juicy seafood simmered in a spicy tomato sauce, served with light rice noodles. If you want a hotter dish, add an extra spoonful of curry paste but remember, you can always add more but you can't take it out!

Serves 4

- 175 g (6 oz) squid, cleaned
- 225 g (8 oz) medium or fine dried rice stick noodles
- 4 tbsp groundnut oil
- 1 red onion, peeled and sliced
- 1 tbsp Thai red curry paste
- 200 g (7 oz) salmon fillet, skinned and cut into 2.5-cm (1-in) cubes
- 500 g (1 lb 2 oz) raw tiger prawns, peeled
- 4 spring onions, trimmed and cut into 2.5-cm (1-in) lengths
- 230-g (8-oz) tin chopped tomatoes
- 2 tbsp light soy sauce
- 1 tbsp Thai fish sauce
- 1 tsp brown sugar
- Fresh mint leaves to garnish

1 Cut the bodies of the squid into 5-cm (2-in) squares and score in a diamond pattern with a sharp knife, taking care not to cut all the way through the flesh. Slice the tentacles into bite-sized pieces.

2 Cook the noodles in a pan of boiling water for 4 minutes (this can be done in a wok or a separate saucepan) or until tender. Drain and keep warm. (Carefully dry the wok if you have used it to cook the noodles.)

3 Heat half the oil in the wok and fry the red onion over a low heat for about 5 minutes until softened. Stir in the curry paste and cook for 1 minute.

4 Add the squid, salmon, prawns and spring onions, increase the heat to medium-high and cook for 3 minutes, stirring regularly. Stir in the tomatoes, soy sauce, fish sauce and sugar and simmer for 3 minutes.

5 Divide the noodles between four serving bowls, ladle over the seafood, scatter over a few mint leaves and serve immediately.

Green Beans with Peppers and Noodles

A tasty supper that tosses Asian noodles with a colourful array of stir-fried vegetables. Serve on its own or as an accompaniment to grilled chops or steaks.

Serves 4

- 250 g (9 oz) dried egg noodles
- 2 tbsp groundnut oil
- 1 red pepper, deseeded and sliced
- 1 yellow pepper, deseeded and sliced
- 2 garlic cloves, peeled and finely chopped
- 1 stalk of lemon grass, finely chopped, or 1 tsp lemon grass purée
- 200 g (7 oz) green beans, trimmed
- 150 g (5 oz) oyster mushrooms, halved
- 3 tbsp light soy sauce
- 1 tsp brown sugar
- 1 tbsp lemon juice
- 1 tbsp sesame seeds

1 Cook the noodles in boiling water according to the packet instructions until tender – this can be done in a wok or a separate pan. Drain and set aside. (Carefully dry the wok if you have used it to cook the noodles.)

2 Heat the oil in the wok and stir-fry the red and yellow peppers, garlic and lemon grass over a high heat for 3 minutes. Add the green beans and mushrooms and stir-fry for 4 minutes.

3 Mix together the soy sauce, sugar and lemon juice. Pour into the wok, add the noodles and toss everything together for 3 minutes or until heated through. Serve sprinkled with the sesame seeds.

> **If you are using the wok to cook the noodles, wipe it out with absorbent kitchen paper so it's completely dry before adding the oil.**

Seafood Paella

Calasparra, the Spanish short-grain rice used to make paella, is so precious it has its own 'denominación de origen' stamp of quality. It can be found in larger supermarkets, but substitute ordinary long-grain rice if it's not available.

Serves 2

- 2 tbsp olive oil
- 1 Spanish onion, peeled and finely sliced
- ½ red pepper, deseeded and chopped
- ½ green pepper, deseeded and chopped
- 175 g (6 oz) Calasparra paella rice
- 85 ml (3 fl oz) dry white wine
- 225 ml (7½ fl oz) fish or vegetable stock
- Few saffron strands
- 75 g (3 oz) frozen peas
- 175 g (6 oz) raw prawns, peeled
- 100 g (4 oz) squid, cleaned, cut into rings/bite-sized pieces
- 500 g (1 lb 2 oz) mussels in their shells, (see page 46 for preparation)
- 2 tbsp chopped fresh parsley

1 Heat the oil in a wok and fry the onion over a low heat for about 10 minutes or until softened. Add the peppers and cook for a further 5 minutes, stirring occasionally.

2 Stir in the rice and cook for 1 minute, then pour in the wine and stock and crumble in the saffron. Bring to the boil, lower the heat and simmer gently for 20–25 minutes or until the rice is almost tender and it has absorbed most of the stock.

3 Stir in the peas, prawns and squid and scatter the mussels over the top. Continue to cook for a further 5–10 minutes or until the rice is tender, the prawns have turned pink and opaque and the mussel shells have opened (discard any that remain closed).

4 Sprinkle with the parsley and serve immediately.

Tofu and Vegetable Stir-fry with Egg Noodles

A treat for vegetarians who can enjoy all the flavours of Oriental food without the addition of meat or fish. Tofu is made from pressed soya beans and is a rich source of protein.

Serves 4

- 175 g (6 oz) dried medium egg noodles
- 75 g (3 oz) blanched almonds
- 250 g (9 oz) firm tofu, cubed
- 3 tbsp plain flour
- 2 tbsp sunflower oil
- 4 baby carrots, scrubbed and quartered lengthways
- 1 red pepper, deseeded and sliced
- 100 g (4 oz) sugar snap peas, halved lengthways
- 1 celery stick, sliced
- 100 g (4 oz) baby corn, each cut into three pieces
- 1 tsp chilli sauce
- 3 tbsp light soy sauce
- 1 tsp cornflour
- 175 ml (6 fl oz) vegetable stock

1 Soak or cook the noodles according to the instructions on the packet. Drain and set aside. Toast the almonds in a dry wok over a medium heat, until golden. Remove to a board and chop. Dust the tofu cubes with the flour. Heat 2 tablespoons of the oil in the wok and stir-fry the cubes over a high heat for 2–3 minutes until golden. Drain and set aside.

2 Add the remaining oil to the wok and stir-fry the carrots over a medium heat for 3 minutes. Add the red pepper, sugar snap peas, celery and baby corn and stir-fry for 5 minutes.

3 In a small bowl, mix together the chilli sauce, soy sauce, cornflour and stock and pour into the wok. Stir until the sauce is smooth and bubbling.

4 Return everything to the wok. Toss together over the heat for 2–3 minutes until coated with the sauce. Serve with the almonds scattered on top.

VEGETABLES

Potato, Pea and Coriander Samosas

These small triangular pasties are a popular street food in India where they are fried in steaming vats of fat on roadside stalls. Serve them hot or cold with a dip of mango chutney or natural yogurt mixed with chopped fresh mint.

Makes 12

Dough

- 225 g (8 oz) plain flour
- ½ tsp salt
- 4 tbsp vegetable oil or ghee (Indian clarified butter), melted
- 100 ml (3½ fl oz) warm (previously boiled) water

Filling

- 500 g (1 lb 2 oz) waxy potatoes
- Vegetable oil for frying
- 2 shallots, peeled and chopped
- 2 garlic cloves, peeled and crushed
- 100 g (4 oz) frozen peas
- 1 tsp cumin seeds
- ½ tsp turmeric
- 3 tbsp chopped fresh coriander

1 To make the dough, sift the flour and salt into a bowl and carefully stir in the oil or ghee. Gradually add the water and mix to a dough.

2 Knead on a floured board until the dough is smooth, wrap in cling film and chill in the fridge for 30 minutes.

3 To make the filling, scrub the unpeeled potatoes and cook in a pan of boiling water (you can use the wok for this if you like) until tender.

4 Drain the potatoes, leave to cool, then peel off the skins and chop them into small dice. (Carefully dry the wok with absorbent kitchen paper if you have used it to boil the potatoes.)

Although the samosas in this recipe are made with ordinary plain flour, in India besan flour (made from chick peas that have been ground to a meal) is often used – or even sometimes a mixture of the two. Indian cooks would also fry the samosas in ghee, a clarified butter that can be heated to high temperatures without burning.

5 Add 2 tablespoons of oil to the wok and, when hot, gently fry the shallots and garlic for 2–3 minutes until soft.

6 Add the potatoes, peas, cumin seeds and turmeric and cook over a medium heat for 3 minutes, stirring frequently. Stir in the coriander and set aside to cool.

7 Remove the dough from the fridge, and divide it into six pieces. Roll one piece to an 18-cm (7-in) round. Cut in half and shape the semi-circles into cones, dampening the edges to seal.

8 Spoon in some of the filling. Dampen the top edge of the dough and press down over the filling, pinching the edges together to seal. Use the remaining dough pieces and filling to make 12 samosas in total.

9 Heat 5 cm (2 in) of oil in the wok to 180°C (350°F) (or until a small cube of bread browns in 40 seconds) and fry the samosas in batches for 3–4 minutes until golden brown all over. Drain on a plate lined with absorbent kitchen paper and serve hot or cold.

Peperonata

A dish of mixed sweet peppers slowly simmered with onions, tomatoes and celery from Piedmont in northern Italy. Serve as a vegetable accompaniment or on its own with grilled polenta or new potatoes.

Serves 4

- 4 tbsp extra-virgin olive oil
- 1 large onion, peeled and finely sliced
- 2 large garlic cloves, peeled and chopped
- 2 red peppers, deseeded and sliced
- 1 yellow pepper, deseeded and sliced
- 2 celery sticks, chopped
- 4 medium ripe tomatoes, peeled and chopped
- 1 tbsp sun-dried tomato purée
- Freshly ground black pepper
- 2 tbsp shredded fresh basil

1 Heat the oil in a wok and fry the onion over a low heat for 10 minutes or until it is soft and starting to turn golden.

2 Add the garlic, peppers and celery and fry for 5 minutes, stirring occasionally.

3 Stir in the tomatoes and sun-dried tomato purée, cover the wok with a lid and simmer for about 30 minutes or until the vegetables are tender. Uncover the wok and simmer for a further 10 minutes so the liquid from the tomatoes reduces.

4 Season with freshly ground black pepper, stir in the basil and serve.

The lazy way to skin the tomatoes is to cut them in half and add them to the wok with the other ingredients. Cover and leave to simmer for about 10 minutes, by which time the skins will have separated from the tomato flesh and they can easily be lifted out. Mash the tomato flesh with a spoon, re-cover the wok and continue.

Root Vegetable and Winter Herb Cakes

Delicious little vegetable cakes that can be prepared in advance. Serve as an accompaniment to sausages, steaks or whatever takes your fancy. Miniature versions of the cakes also make good party food served with a dipping sauce.

Serves 4

- 225 g (8 oz) sweet potatoes
- 225 g (8 oz) potatoes
- Sunflower oil for frying
- 1 onion, peeled and finely chopped
- 225 g (8 oz) carrots, peeled and grated
- 2 tsp fresh thyme leaves
- 2 tsp chopped fresh rosemary
- Plain flour, to dust
- 1 egg, beaten
- 50 g (2 oz) fresh breadcrumbs

1 Scrub the unpeeled sweet potatoes and ordinary potatoes and cook in a pan of boiling water (this can be done in the wok) until tender when pierced with a skewer. Drain and, when the potatoes are cool enough to handle, peel, place in a bowl and coarsely crush with a fork. (Carefully dry the wok if you have used it to cook the potatoes.)

2 Heat 2 tablespoons of oil in the wok and fry the onion over a low heat for 5 minutes. Stir in the carrots, thyme and rosemary and cook for 2 minutes. Add to the crushed potatoes and stir until mixed.

3 Leave to cool and then shape the mixture into 8 round flat cakes. Dust with flour, brush with beaten egg and coat in the breadcrumbs. Chill for about 1 hour to firm up.

4 Heat 2.5 cm/1 in of oil in the wok and
fry the cakes in two batches. Fry each
batch for about 5 minutes, until golden
brown on both sides, turning over
halfway through cooking. Drain on a plate
lined with absorbent kitchen paper and
serve hot.

> **Crushing rather than
> mashing the potatoes gives
> the cakes a more interesting
> texture when you bite into
> them.**

Steamed Baby Pak Choi with Garlic

An attractive side dish of colourful vegetables tossed in a fresh lemon and light soy sauce. Serve it with seafood or chicken stir-fries.

Serves 4

- 500 g (1 lb 2 oz) baby pak choi
- 1 tbsp vegetable oil
- 2 garlic cloves, peeled and thinly sliced
- 4 spring onions, trimmed and cut into 2.5-cm (1-in) lengths
- 100 g (4 oz) button mushrooms, halved
- 6 cherry tomatoes, quartered
- 2 tbsp lemon juice
- 2 tbsp light soy sauce
- ¼ tsp caster sugar

> **Keep the heads of pak choi whole and take care not to steam them for too long. The leaves should be tender but the stalks should still have a little crunch.**

1 Arrange the pak choi on a steaming rack. Fill a wok one-third full with hot water, place the rack in position and cover with a lid. Steam the pack choi for 3–4 minutes until tender. Drain, transfer to a serving dish and keep warm.

2 Pour the water out of the wok and carefully wipe it dry. Add the oil and gently fry the garlic until golden. Drain and set aside.

3 Add the spring onions and mushrooms to the wok and stir-fry over a high heat for 2 minutes. Add the tomato quarters and stir-fry for 1 minute.

4 Add the lemon juice, soy sauce and sugar and stir until the vegetables are coated. Spoon them over the pak choi, sprinkle over the garlic and serve immediately.

Chilli Stir-fried Vegetables

A rainbow mix of fresh vegetables tossed with Chinese egg noodles and a tangy sauce makes a meat-free meal for two that can be cooked in minutes. If you prefer, leave out the noodles and serve with boiled rice instead.

Serves 2

- 2 tbsp sunflower oil
- 1 carrot, peeled and cut into julienne
- 1 small red pepper, deseeded and sliced
- 75 g (3 oz) mushrooms, halved or quartered
- 75 g (3 oz) baby corn, halved
- 50 g (2 oz) mangetout, halved lengthways
- 4 spring onions, trimmed and cut into 2.5-cm (1-in) lengths
- 225 g (8 oz) fresh Chinese egg noodles
- 2 tbsp light soy sauce
- 2 tsp sweet chilli sauce
- 1 tbsp balsamic vinegar

1 Heat the oil in a wok, add the carrot and stir-fry over a high heat for 3 minutes. Add the red pepper, mushrooms and baby corn and stir-fry for 3 minutes.

2 Add the mangetout and spring onions, stir-fry for 2 minutes and then toss in the noodles.

3 Mix together the soy sauce, chilli sauce and balsamic vinegar and pour into the wok. Stir-fry for 2 minutes until the vegetables and noodles are coated in the sauces and everything is piping hot.

4 Pile on to serving plates or into bowls and serve immediately.

Balti Vegetables with Mango

A medium-hot curry packed with bright vegetables and sweet mango. Serve with pilau rice (see the box below) and naan bread.

Serves 4

- 8 new potatoes, halved
- 2 carrots, peeled and sliced
- 175 g (6 oz) small cauliflower florets
- 2 tbsp vegetable oil
- 1 onion, peeled and chopped
- 1 courgette, trimmed and chopped
- 1 red pepper, deseeded and chopped
- 2 tbsp balti curry paste
- 1 tsp chilli powder or paste
- 200 ml (7 fl oz) vegetable stock
- 225-g (8-oz) tin chopped tomatoes
- 1 mango, peeled and flesh chopped
- 2 tbsp chopped fresh coriander

1 Fill a wok one-third full with water and bring to the boil. Add the potatoes and carrots and cook for 5 minutes. Add the cauliflower florets and cook for a further 3 minutes, then drain. Carefully wipe the wok dry.

2 Heat the oil in the wok and fry the onion over a low heat for 5 minutes until softened. Add the courgette, red pepper, potatoes, carrots and cauliflower and fry for 3 minutes, stirring occasionally.

3 Stir in the curry paste and chilli, cook for 1 minute then pour in the stock and tomatoes. Lower the heat, cover and simmer for 15 minutes or until the vegetables are tender.

4 Stir in the mango and simmer for 2–3 minutes or until heated through. Serve sprinkled with the coriander.

Pilau rice can be cooked in a wok. For four servings, gently fry 225 g (8 oz) basmati rice in 50 g (2 oz) melted butter for 3 minutes until the rice grains are translucent. Stir in 750 ml (1¼ pt) vegetable stock, cover with a lid and cook over a very low heat, without disturbing the rice, for about 15 minutes or until the water has been absorbed and the rice is tender. Remove the lid and put a clean cloth over the surface of the rice. Leave to stand for 15 minutes to dry the grains. Reheat in a covered dish in a moderate oven for 10–15 minutes when ready to serve.

Thai Green Vegetable Curry

A creamy mild curry packed with colourful vegetables and flavoured with coconut milk. Instead of rice, serve with warm puffs of naan bread.

Serves 4

- 2 tbsp vegetable oil
- 175 g (6 oz) baby carrots, scrubbed
- 1 onion, peeled and chopped
- 175 g (6 oz) (prepared weight) butternut squash, peeled, deseeded and cut into chunks
- 175 g (6 oz) cauliflower florets
- 1 red pepper, deseeded and chopped
- 2 tbsp Thai green curry paste
- 200 ml (7 fl oz) vegetable stock
- 300 ml (½ pt) coconut milk
- 150 g (5 oz) spinach leaves, shredded
- Naan bread, to serve

1 Heat the oil in a wok, add the baby carrots and chopped onion and fry over a medium heat for 5 minutes. Add the chunks of squash, cauliflower florets and red pepper and fry for a further 5 minutes, stirring occasionally.

2 Stir in the curry paste and cook for 1 minute then pour in the stock. Lower the heat, cover the wok and simmer for 25 minutes or until the vegetables are tender.

3 Stir in the coconut milk and spinach and simmer for 2–3 minutes or until the spinach wilts. Serve with warm naan bread.

> **Once you've added the coconut milk don't let the curry boil hard or the sauce will separate and become oily. Leave it to simmer over a gentle heat until the spinach is cooked and the sauce piping hot.**

Feta, Red Pepper and Mint Filos

Usually filled with spinach, these crisp, tasty little parcels ring the changes with a colourful mix of red pepper, fresh mint and tangy feta cheese. Serve with a salad of tomato, olives and cucumber with olive oil and balsamic vinegar.

Serves 4

- Olive oil for frying
- 2 shallots or large spring onions, peeled and finely chopped
- 2 red peppers, deseeded and finely chopped
- 175 g (6 oz) feta cheese, crumbled
- 1 tbsp finely chopped fresh mint
- 6 sheets of filo pastry
- 1 egg white, lightly beaten
- 1 tbsp cumin, poppy or sesame seeds (optional)

1 Heat 1 tablespoon of olive oil in a wok and fry the shallots or spring onions and red peppers over a low heat for 7–8 minutes or until softened. Transfer to a bowl and leave to cool, then mix in the feta and mint. Carefully wipe out the wok with absorbent kitchen paper.

2 Cut one sheet of filo in half lengthways to give two long strips. Spoon a little of the pepper mixture at one end of a filo strip.

3 Brush the edges of the filo with beaten egg white, fold the corner of the pastry over the filling to make a triangle and continue folding all the way up the strip, sealing the parcel by pressing the pastry edges together. Repeat using the rest of the filo and filling to make 12 parcels.

4 Brush the top of the parcels with egg white and sprinkle over the cumin or sesame seeds, if using.

5 Heat 2.5 cm (1 in) of oil in the wok and fry the parcels three or four at a time, about 5 minutes each batch or until golden brown and crisp on both sides. Drain on absorbent kitchen paper and serve hot.

To use a spinach filling, substitute 250 g (9 oz) cooked chopped spinach for the red peppers. Drain the spinach well though, so there is no excess moisture; if it is too damp, the moisture will make the filo pastry soggy rather than crisp and flaky.

Omelette Rolls with Sweet and Sour Vegetables

The bright selection of vegetables makes an attractive filling for the golden egg rolls. After stir-frying, the vegetables should still be slightly crisp so their crunch make a good contrast to the soft omelette wrap when you bite into them.

Serves 4

- 3 tbsp groundnut or sunflower oil
- 1 red pepper, deseeded and chopped
- 150 g (5 oz) tenderstem broccoli, chopped
- 1 large carrot, peeled and grated
- 75 g (3 oz) mangetout, sliced thinly lengthways
- 75 g (3 oz) mushrooms, chopped or sliced
- 3 tinned water chestnuts, chopped
- 50 g (2 oz) bean sprouts
- 3 tbsp rice vinegar
- 1 tbsp clear honey
- 3 tbsp light soy sauce, and extra for dipping
- 2 tbsp tomato ketchup
- 4 large eggs

1 Heat 2 tablespoons of the oil in a wok, add the red pepper and broccoli and stir-fry for 3 minutes over a fairly high heat. Add the carrot, mangetout, mushrooms, water chestnuts and bean sprouts and stir-fry for a further 3 minutes.

2 In a small bowl, whisk together the vinegar, honey, soy sauce and ketchup and pour into the wok. Toss the vegetables until they are coated in the sauce, then transfer to a plate and keep warm in a low oven.

3 Carefully rinse out the wok and wipe it dry with absorbent kitchen paper. Place over a moderate heat and add the remaining 1 tablespoon oil.

4 Beat one egg in a jug or cup and pour it into the wok. Tilt the pan so the egg spreads in a thin layer over the base and part way up the sides and cook for about 1 minute or until the egg is just set in a thin omelette. Remove from the pan

and make three more omelettes in the same way.

5 Place an omelette on each plate, divide the vegetables between them and roll up. Cut into slices and serve warm with a bowl of soy sauce for dipping.

Ordinary broccoli could be used instead of tenderstem, but then it is best to cut the head into small florets and blanch them for a couple of minutes in boiling water, or steam them on a rack in the wok. This tenderizes the stalks.

Spicy Sweetcorn Patties

These can be served with a mixed salad as a lunch or supper dish, or with a bowl of sweet and sour sauce, peanut sauce or lemon mayonnaise for dipping as an unusual party food to serve with drinks.

Serves 4

- 75 g (3 oz) fine green beans, finely chopped
- ½ red pepper, deseeded and finely chopped
- 4 spring onions, finely chopped
- 100 g (4 oz) sweetcorn kernels
- 1 tbsp Thai red curry paste
- 1 tbsp light soy sauce
- 1 tsp brown sugar
- 1 tbsp chopped fresh parsley
- 75 g (3 oz) plain flour
- 1 egg, beaten
- Vegetable oil for frying

To garnish
- Shredded spring onions
- Fine slices of red chilli
- Fresh parsley sprigs

1 Place the green beans, red pepper and spring onions in a bowl with the sweetcorn and stir in the curry paste, soy sauce, sugar and chopped parsley.

2 Add the flour and stir until all the vegetables are coated, then beat in the egg so the ingredients bind together.

3 Heat 2.5 cm (1 in) of oil in a wok and carefully drop dessertspoonfuls of the mixture into the hot oil. Fry in batches for 3–4 minutes until the patties are golden brown. Drain on a plate lined with absorbent kitchen paper and serve hot garnished with shredded spring onions, fine slices of red chilli and parsley sprigs.

Use Thai green curry paste if you prefer or an Indian spice mix such as masala or korma. If using canned sweetcorn kernels, drain them thoroughly before mixing with the rest of the vegetables.

Vegetable Pakoras with Yogurt and Mint Dip

A traditional Indian snack that can be served as part of a spread of different dishes or as finger food. As with the samosas (page 158), Indian cooks would make the batter with besan (chick pea flour), but plain wholemeal flour is used here.

Serves 4

Dip
- 5 tbsp thick natural yogurt
- 2 tbsp chopped fresh mint
- ½ tsp paprika

Pakoras
- 250 g (9 oz) plain wholemeal flour, plus extra for dusting
- Pinch of salt
- 2 tsp ground coriander
- 1 tsp black onion seeds
- 2 tbsp finely chopped fresh coriander
- About 500 ml (18 fl oz) cold water
- 8 baby carrots, scrubbed
- ½ cauliflower, divided into small florets
- 200 g (7 oz) broccoli, divided into small florets
- 2 egg whites
- Vegetable oil for frying
- 8 chestnut mushrooms

1 To make the dip, mix the yogurt and 1 tablespoon mint together and spoon into a serving bowl. Scatter the rest of the mint and the paprika on top and chill until needed.

2 To make the pakoras, mix together the flour, salt, ground coriander, onion seeds and fresh coriander in a bowl. Make a well in the centre of the dry ingredients and add enough cold water to make a smooth batter that has the consistency of unwhipped double cream. Leave the batter to stand for 1 hour or until you are ready to fry the vegetables.

3 Meanwhile, steam the carrots, cauliflower and broccoli on a steaming rack over boiling water in the wok, with the lid on, for 5–10 minutes or until the vegetables feel just tender when pierced with the point of a sharp knife. Remove the vegetables from the rack and leave them to cool. Drain off the water from the

wok and carefully wipe it out with absorbent kitchen paper until it is completely dry.

4 Whisk the egg whites until standing in soft peaks and fold into the batter with a large metal spoon.

5 Heat about 2.5 cm (1 in) of oil in the wok. Dust all the vegetables, including the mushrooms, with flour

and add them to the batter, turning them over until well coated. Lift out the vegetables one at a time so they don't stick together and add them to the hot oil. Fry in batches for 2–3 minutes until crisp and deep golden brown.

6 Drain the vegetables on to a plate lined with absorbent kitchen paper and serve hot with the dip.

Mushroom Medley in a Creamy Saffron Sauce

A creamy mix of mushrooms given a golden hue by the addition of crumbled saffron strands to the sauce. Serve as a vegetable accompaniment to meat, poultry and fish dishes or as a vegetarian dish spooned over rice or soft polenta.

Serves 4

- Few saffron strands
- 3 tbsp olive oil
- 1 red onion, peeled and chopped
- 1 green pepper, peeled and chopped
- 1 red pepper, peeled and chopped
- 1 courgette, trimmed and chopped
- 1 tsp fresh thyme leaves
- 150 g (5 oz) baby button mushrooms
- 150 g (5 oz) shiitake mushrooms, sliced
- 150 g (5 oz) enoki, shimeji or other small Oriental mushroom
- 200 ml (7 fl oz) crème fraîche
- Freshly ground black pepper

1 Crumble the saffron strands into a small bowl and add 2 tablespoons of boiling water. Leave to soak.

2 Heat half the olive oil in a wok, add the onion and fry over a low heat for 5 minutes until softened. Add the green pepper, red pepper, courgette and thyme and fry for 4 minutes.

3 Add all the mushrooms and stir in the saffron and its soaking liquid. Cover and simmer for 5 minutes.

4 Stir in the crème fraîche and plenty of freshly ground black pepper and heat through for 1 minute. Serve hot.

> **Saffron is the world's most expensive spice, but luckily only a few strands are needed. You could add a teaspoon of turmeric instead, but the dish will then have a mild curry flavour.**

Crushed Potatoes with Shredded Cabbage and Leeks

Bubble and squeak in a wok makes a feel-good accompaniment to comfort foods like sausages, bacon and baked beans. The dish can be made with leftover potatoes.

Serves 4

- 700 g (1½ lb) floury potatoes, boiled until just tender
- 4 tbsp olive oil
- 75 g (3 oz) butter
- 2 leeks, trimmed and thinly sliced
- ¼ green cabbage (e.g. Savoy), shredded
- Freshly ground black pepper
- 2 tbsp snipped fresh chives
- 2 tbsp chopped fresh parsley

> **When breaking up the potatoes, take care to leave them in small chunks rather than reducing them to a smooth mash.**

1 Break up and coarsely crush the potatoes with a fork.

2 Heat half the oil and butter in a wok, add the leeks and cabbage and cover with the lid. Cook over a low heat for 4–5 minutes until the vegetables have softened, then remove and set aside.

3 Add the rest of the oil and butter to the wok and when foaming, tip in the potatoes. Fry, uncovered, over a medium heat for about 10 minutes, turning the potatoes over regularly so they brown evenly.

4 When they are golden, return the leeks and cabbage to the wok, stir well to mix them with the potatoes and cook for 1 minute.

5 Season with freshly ground black pepper and serve with the chives and parsley scattered over.

Bean and Vegetable Pot

Thick and warming with lots of contrasting textures and flavours, this rich bean and vegetable stew is the perfect feel-good food for a cold winter's day.

Serves 4

- 2 tbsp sunflower oil
- 25 g (1 oz) butter
- 1 leek, trimmed and thinly sliced
- 150 g (5 oz) carrots, peeled and chopped
- 200 g (7 oz) (prepared weight) butternut squash, peeled and cut into small chunks
- 300 ml (½ pt) tomato juice
- 300 ml (½ pt) vegetable stock
- 230-g (8-oz) tin chopped tomatoes
- 400-g (14-oz) tin cannellini beans, drained and rinsed
- 400-g (14-oz) tin flageolet beans, drained and rinsed
- 3 tbsp chopped fresh parsley

1 Heat the oil and butter in a wok, add the leek, carrots and squash, cover and cook over a low heat for 10 minutes, stirring occasionally.

2 Add the tomato juice, stock and tomatoes and bring to a simmer. Re-cover the wok and cook for 20 minutes or until the vegetables are tender.

3 Add the cannellini and flageolet beans and simmer for 10 minutes. Serve with the parsley sprinkled over.

Serve with thick slices of toasted French bread, spread with mild mustard, topped with a mixture of grated Cheddar and Parmesan cheeses and grilled until the cheese melts.

Asparagus, Mushrooms and Green Beans in Rosemary Oil

A light, aromatic side dish that can be served straight from the wok as an accompaniment to roast pork or lamb. Alternatively, leave the vegetables to go cold and serve as a summer salad.

Serves 4

- 500 g (1 lb 2 oz) asparagus spears, trimmed
- 150 g (5 oz) green beans, trimmed
- 4 tbsp extra-virgin olive oil
- 1 tbsp finely chopped fresh rosemary
- 1 courgette, cut into julienne
- 100 g (4 oz) mushrooms, quartered or sliced
- 2 tbsp lemon juice
- Freshly ground black pepper

1 Fill a wok one-third full with water and bring to the boil. Spread out the asparagus on a steaming rack, place in position in the wok, cover and steam for 3 minutes. Add the green beans to the rack and steam for a further 2 minutes or until the asparagus is just tender.

2 Remove the vegetables from the rack and pour the water out of the wok. Carefully wipe the wok dry, place it over a medium heat and add the olive oil and rosemary. Stir-fry the courgette and mushrooms for 2 minutes.

3 Add the asparagus and green beans and stir-fry for a further 2 minutes. Sprinkle over the lemon juice, season with plenty of freshly ground black pepper and serve.

As different types of asparagus vary in size you may need to increase or reduce the steaming time according to the thickness of the spears. They should be just tender when pierced with the point of a sharp knife, not soggy or starting to collapse.

Cauliflower with Tomatoes, Shallots and Courgettes

A more interesting way of serving cauliflower than coating it in the ubiquitous cheese sauce. The combination of frying and steaming makes it an ideal dish for cooking in a wok.

Serves 4

- 1 cauliflower
- 2 tbsp sunflower oil
- 3 shallots, peeled and chopped
- 2 small courgettes, trimmed and chopped
- 2 medium tomatoes, diced
- 150 ml (¼ pt) vegetable stock
- Freshly ground black pepper
- 1 tsp fresh thyme leaves

1 Cut away the tough stalk from the cauliflower and divide the head into small florets.

2 Heat the oil in a wok and fry the shallots over a low heat for 5 minutes until softened but not browned. Add the cauliflower florets and courgettes and fry for 2 minutes, stirring occasionally.

3 Add the tomatoes and stock, put the lid on the wok and simmer for 5–8 minutes or until the cauliflower is tender. Season with freshly ground black pepper, sprinkle over the thyme leaves and serve as an accompaniment to roast beef, pork or lamb.

The length of simmering time will depend on the size of the cauliflower florets – they're ready when the thickest part of the stem is just tender when pierced with the point of a sharp knife.

Index

190